PRAISE FOR
YOU DON'T HAVE TO CARRY IT ALL

"Paula pulls back the curtain to reveal the truth and double standards that women face in the workplace, especially after becoming moms. She shares the real story behind the statistics and makes those of us who have experienced the challenges and obstacles we face feel seen and heard.

Relatable, realistic, yet revolutionary, Paula speaks with candor and humor. You can feel the pain and bewilderment that led her to write this book not only to make sense of her own experience but to challenge the norms that brought her here. She calls on us to end mom guilt and the feeling we have to carry it all, and instead learn to support one another and extend each other grace and support. A must-read for mothers in the workplace."

—*Deb Liu*, CEO of Ancestry.com, author, and mom of three

"Paula is one of those women who seems to have it all—while effortlessly doing it all, without breaking a sweat or breaking a nail. You just can't imagine her in a pair of Spanx.

Well, the real Paula is not that woman at all and she willingly admits it. With gut-level honesty and good-natured humor, Paula shares her frustrations and desperations over being a working mother in her latest book.

She uses her unique skills as a journalist and interviewer to take you along on her journey. And hopefully share some powerful guidance and advice on how you can begin to put down all the baggage and actually take control of your life again."

—*Kathie Lee Gifford*, Emmy Award–winning co-host
and *New York Times* bestselling author

"For years, I've had a front-row seat to watch my wife, Amy, juggle the demands of her ministry, her profession, her friendships, and our family with six children. Like Amy, many of us feel like it's impossible to do everything that matters to us. Thankfully, my good friend Paula Faris has written a deeply encouraging and profoundly practical book called *You Don't Have to Carry It All*. In her book, Paula shares the raw and unfiltered truth of her personal journey alongside doable and life-changing advice that will encourage and equip readers to let go of their guilt and live a life focused on what truly matters."

—*Craid Groeschel*, pastor of Life.Church and
New York Times bestselling author

"With the many demands and competing priorities that working mothers experience, we can easily run ourselves into burnout and isolation. Paula reminds us that we are not alone, and that together, we have the power to create meaningful and lasting change."

—*Danielle Walker*, *New York Times* bestselling author of the
Against All Grain series

"This book is a game-changer for working moms. A must-read!"

—*Shawn Johnson East*, Olympic gymnast, bestselling author,
CEO, and mom

"THIS is the book working moms have been waiting for! In *You Don't Have to Carry It All*, Paula shows us how to create meaningful change and finally put an end to mom guilt."

—*Jenna Bush Hager*, co-host of *TODAY with Hoda & Jenna*
and founder, Read With Jenna

"*You Don't Have to Carry It All* explores the challenges that working mothers face from so many thoughtful and insightful angles. You will be both encouraged and motivated to action by this empathetic and empowering book."

—*Dr. Anita Phillips*, trauma therapist and host of the *In the Light* podcast

you don't have to

CARRY IT ALL

you don't have to CARRY IT ALL

DITCH THE MOM GUILT AND FIND A BETTER WAY FORWARD

PAULA FARIS

With Holly Crawshaw

New York • Nashville

Worthy

Hachette Book Group

1290 Avenue of the Americas, New York, NY 10104

worthypublishing.com

twitter.com/worthypub

First Edition: March 2023

Worthy is a division of Hachette Book Group, Inc. The Worthy name and logo are trademarks of Hachette Book Group, Inc.

The publisher is not responsible for websites (or their content) that are not owned by the publisher.

Unless otherwise noted, Scripture quotations are taken from the Holy Bible, New International Version®. Copyright © 1973, 1978, 1984, 2011 by Biblica, Inc.™ Used by permission of Zondervan. All rights reserved worldwide. www.zondervan.com. The "NIV" and "New International Version" are trademarks registered in the United States Patent and Trademark Office by Biblica, Inc.™

Worthy Books may be purchased in bulk for business, educational, or promotional use. For information, please contact your local bookseller or the Hachette Book Group Special Markets Department at special.markets@hbgusa.com.

Print book interior design by Bart Dawson.

Library of Congress Cataloging-in-Publication Data

Names: Faris, Paula, 1975- author.

Title: You don't have to carry it all : ditch the mom guilt and find a better way forward / Paula Faris.

Description: First edition. | Nashville : Worthy, [2023] | Summary: "Being a working mom should work. Instead, it is a thankless, incredibly difficult job, marked by impossible contradictions and unreachable expectations. American moms are more burned out than any time in history. We believed we could have it all - fulfilling work and a healthy and happy family. We pick up responsibilities wherever we go - at work, at home, in our communities. We try to CARRY it all-and we can. Because moms are superheroes with superpowers! But at some point, our shoulders grow tired - tired from carrying around the expectations and the mental load, tired from juggling the constant conflict between working and momming, tired of how our work - whether at home or at the office - isn't valued equally, and tired of workplaces that treat us like risks instead of assets. Award-winning journalist and mom-of-three Paula Faris offers a declaration to the millions of overwhelmed and depleted working moms out there - things ARE going to get better! There is another way forward that frees us from the barbaric conflict of mom-guilt and the bone-weary exhaustion of carrying it all and feeling like we're failing everywhere. Through the lens of her personal experience and interviews with working women, men, leaders and experts across the country, Faris dismantles the cultural expectations and toxic traps that American moms experience. She also gathers insightful and actionable steps towards a better way of working, momming, and living. The problems we have as a country and culture are not insurmountable. Besides, we've got working moms on this job. And there are literally no hands more capable than ours!"-- Provided by publisher.

Identifiers: LCCN 2022047943 | ISBN 9781546003731 (hardcover) | ISBN 9781546003755 (ebook)

Subjects: LCSH: Working mothers. | Work and family. | Career development. | Work-life balance.

Classification: LCC HQ759.48 .F37 2023 | DDC 331.4/4--dc23/eng/20221116

LC record available at https://lccn.loc.gov/2022047943

ISBNs: 978-1-5460-0373-1 (hardcover), 978-1-5460-0375-5 (ebook)

Printed in the United States of America

LSC-C

Printing 1, 2022

To all moms, future moms, and brave dads…
(Without you, our society ceases to exist.
Don't ever forget that!)
Telling your stories is the most important
reporting I'll ever do.
May these pages give you hope,
knowing there is a better way forward.

CONTENTS

INTRODUCTION

Someone in their 20s asked me recently, "What do you do?"

Simple enough question, right?

However, since I left my job at ABC News in 2020, I truly struggle to answer it.

Am I a stay-at-home mom with a side hustle? Am I an independent contractor, an entrepreneur? A washed-up former network news anchor?

What I do know is that I'm more confident than ever about my mission in this season, which is to change the game for moms on their workplace journey.

You see, I lost my job as a journalist and media personality at the beginning of the pandemic, when I was not re-signed by the network. This massive change in my life and career forced me to figure out what I wanted next. Get another job in TV, which seemed like the safe choice? Or blow up my life, move to a small town in South Carolina, and start

> You see, I lost my job as a journalist and media personality at the beginning of the pandemic, when I was not re-signed by the network.

a company to give working moms a voice, all while draining my retirement account to get it off the ground?

I chose the latter. What can I say? I like risk. And I like to advocate for moms.

On the other side of eviction is an invitation (thank you for that line, Glennon Doyle).

And the invitation for me was to form and found CARRY Media, which is dedicated to handing working moms the microphone. To tell her story in order to enact change. To provide content and resources to help *carry* her load. We are the only media company committed to telling the story of the 35 million moms in the workplace (give or take a few million, thanks to the pandemic, childcare, and the workplace *not* working for moms).

As a mom of three kiddos, I've always worked. But I've always felt torn. And I've never in the history of my time as a mama ever felt like I was nailing it.

- Burnout? Check.
- The constant juggle and mental load? Check.
- Conflict between working and momming? Check.
- Gender pay disparity? Unfortunately, check.
- Being treated like a liability because I was a mom? Don't get me started.

Being a working mom should work. But today in America, it doesn't.

To the mamas and hopeful mamas (brave dads, too) reading this book, *this* is the book I wish someone had written for me to help me navigate work and motherhood.

This book is a hug. It's a declaration that things are going to get better. That we shouldn't have to choose between working and momming. And it's my promise to beat the hell out of the drum for you.

I want to change the game for working moms and, ultimately, for families.

We're treated like a liability. We're punished for actually furthering society. Think about it for a hot second: what happens if we stop having kids? Society is gone. Buh-bye. How ridiculous is this reality?

And it is a reality. Moms make 70 percent of what dads do.[1] We're penalized once we have kids (the mom penalty), and God forbid we take some time away to raise our kids and have a "mommy gap" on the ol' resume.

> Moms make 70% of what dads do.

Maybe, just maybe, corporate America, culture, and society should start celebrating us instead of scrutinizing us.

And maybe, just maybe, we could figure out a way to lose the mom guilt in the process. I'm down with that.

My husband says I can be "a bit much." If you're familiar with the Enneagram, I'm an 8. Essentially that means I like to challenge and disrupt. You want to get it done? I'm your girl.

And what am I backing it up with? Hundreds of interviews. Hard-core facts. Science and research.

I interviewed men and women of different races, socioeconomic statuses, political affiliations, and faiths, and we all agree that there are significant systemic roadblocks harming American families that can be traced back to how our country and its corporations treat working moms.

I have experienced it. My friends have experienced it. The strangers I connected with all over the country have experienced it.

My experience in the workplace and finding out what other mamas are dealing with has set me on a journey to get answers. And I'm taking you with me. As a journalist and storyteller, this is one of the most important stories I'll ever tell.

So to answer that lovely 20-something's question: what do I do? Well, I'm learning I don't have to carry it all. And neither do you.

All you have to do is read, and then act. And I've made it as easy as possible for you. Working moms have no free time. My team and I at CARRY Media like to say that you get about fourteen minutes a day to yourself.

Fourteen.

This book is divided into ten chapters. Within those chapters are sections with boldface subtitles. Each section should take you no more than fourteen minutes to read.

If you will give me your "spare" time, I will give American moms a game plan for how to ditch mom guilt, discover your superpowers, and find a better way forward.

CHAPTER ONE

THE CARRY-ALL

How parents are treated and held and protected and supported is the greatest reflection of a nation. Because how we parent is the foundation of everything: what we value, what we stand for, who we are, and who we're becoming.

—Amy Henderson, author and founder of TendLab

"Mom, how old are you in dog years?"

The question from my youngest child came while I was driving him to baseball practice. Landon reminds me a lot of myself... asking *so* many questions. But big, deep questions. Ones like, "Would you rather live without the sun or the moon?" and "Would you rather live in Earth's gravity or zero gravity?" Questions that legit make my head hurt.

As I watched the road in front of us, I took a moment to do the math in my head, which these days is a bit fried from mothering.

"I'm approximately 330 years in dog years," I told Landon.

And y'all…I feel every bit of it, too.

My guess is that if you're a mom in America, you're feeling every bit of it as well. A tad crispy, fried, or burned out.

Research done by CARRY Media shows close to *90 percent* of working mamas in America are feeling some level of burnout. Then there's the whole mommy gap, mom punishment, and the reality that moms are treated like risks and liabilities in the workforce.

In fact, as I'm writing this book, I've called a therapist for the first time in years, because I feel like I'm at the end of the end of the end of myself.

My dear friend Jo Saxton says that's exactly how you describe being burned out.

You may not be burned out on a job. I actually love being an entrepreneur, hustling on my side gigs, recording podcasts in my basement…

But I'm burned out on motherhood.

I'm burned out on mom guilt.

I'm burned out on the expectations—my own and others'.

There. I said it. I am completely burned out on being a mom.

When I pumped the brakes back in 2018 at the height of my career, anchoring *Good Morning America* and co-hosting *The View*, I was burned out. I wrote about it in my memoir, *Called Out*. Feeling like I was never nailing it, feeling like I should have been momming when I was working and working when I was momming, and feeling every bit of the strain of society not valuing mothers in the workforce. So, I stepped into a much less prestigious position at ABC, demoting myself.

Then my circumstances at the network changed in 2020 when

they chose not to re-sign me. As happened to so many mothers, the pandemic pushed me out of a job I had worked hard to achieve.

What did I do next? Like so many of you, I moved.

My family and I relocated to South Carolina, where I had a midlife crisis that involved joining a CrossFit gym, getting my concealed weapons permit, going on Prozac, and buying a Jeep Wrangler.

And guess what? I'm still burned out.

Why is it so hard to be a working mom in America?

Well, that's one reason I decided to write this book.

To encourage you and remind me that *you don't have to carry it all.*

Sure, you can. And you probably do. That bag on the cover of this book? I've been carrying it. You have, too. Ladies, it's *heavy.* And overflowing. Let's put it down for a moment.

What if we could ditch the mom guilt, beat burnout, and find a new way forward?

I'm down for that.

Are you? I invite you to join me on this journey.

OVERFLOW

If you're a working mother in America, I'd bet that at some point you've encountered righteous frustration. We pick up responsibilities wherever we go—because we're supposed to, right? At work, at home, in our communities. And we endeavor to carry it all—figuratively and literally.

If you're like me, you and your family could live off the contents of your purse for a handful of days. It's not a carry-all bag in name only. We fill our purses the same way we fill our lives—to overflow. We try to carry it all.

But eventually our shoulders grow tired. We don't want to be seen as uncommitted, so we take on that extra project, even though it means cutting into family time.

Our arms become weak. We don't want to be the only mom who doesn't show up for a parent-teacher conference at school, so we contort ourselves like acrobats to fit in all the pieces of our calendar's puzzle together. Ah, thank you #MomGuilt.

It's impossible to be all things to all people.

When I was still working at ABC News, I came across an article in *The Atlantic* called "It's Almost Impossible to Be a Mom in Television News."[1] It shared statistics that shook me. Things like once a woman becomes a mother, she is likely to earn less. If a prospective employee reveals that she is a mother in the interview process, she is less likely to be offered a job. When mothers are late for work, they're more likely to be judged harshly.

The article noted what I and so many of my colleagues and friends had lived: Being a working mom in America is a thankless, incredibly difficult job, marked by impossible contradictions and unreachable expectations. The piece also suggested that a woman can't have a career in news television *and* a family she invests in well.

> Being a working mom in America is a thankless, incredibly difficult job, marked by impossible contradictions and unreachable expectations.

To be clear, that news article didn't shake me in a this-can't-be-true way. I was shaken in a someone-is-*finally*-saying-this way.

When I told my boss that a lot of the

women in the office were talking about it, he unofficially tasked me with researching what the pain points were in being a mother and working at the network. So that's what I did. Over a dozen interviews and fourteen pages of research later, I learned that *every single one of us is asked to carry it all.*

THE CARRY-ALL CYCLE

The entities we work for are not the only ones asking for us to carry it all. Our culture also asks us to carry it all. And when we drop something that we've been carrying, we're either weak or a failure.

Today's all-digital-all-the-time posture has sadly normalized comparison—women compare themselves and their lives to things and people they see online. Science says that women are much more likely than men to fall into the comparison trap.[2] The same study found that women are more likely to fantasize about their lives mirroring the images they see on social media. Why?

Probably because we're desperately trying to figure out how everyone else is doing it and carrying it all while we feel like our own lives are such a dumpster fire.

It's an assault to our self-image every time we scroll. We swipe and see a precious sleeping baby curled up in a hospital bed in the sweetest outfit that matches Mommy's—who, by the way, posted a #KeepingItReal photo of her post-baby body while *still* in the hospital. She's only got eight more pounds to go! "Breastfeeding has been an incredible journey so far," she writes, but making sure she adds "But FED is BEST!" to remain inclusive.

Meanwhile, we're home with mastitis for the tenth time, a

bra full of wilted cabbage (been there, done that), a toddler we can't wean, an elementary schooler with math homework we don't understand, massaging our sore boobs while trying to decide what's for dinner: chicken or chicken? Oh, and, by the way, our boss just scheduled a mandatory Zoom meeting for the exact time we're supposed to do carpool tomorrow.

No wonder we feel like we're failing. No wonder we feel like we can't measure up. The working mom in America has no realistic measuring stick to compare ourselves to. There is no "balance," there is no checklist, there is no way to know if we're passing or failing. We're just told to carry it all. So we wake up, pick up our responsibilities—the real ones and perceived ones—and trudge slowly to the finish line of bedtime, where we lie awake in order to have just a few precious moments to ourselves.

> The working mom in America has no realistic measuring stick to compare ourselves to.

And then we wake up and do it all again.

GOING SOUTH

When the COVID-19 pandemic hit in 2020, my real estate investor husband and I had recently bought an investment property in a small town in South Carolina where my sister was living. The idea was to use it as a vacation rental while we were in New York and to maybe stay a month or so every summer.

As I was exiting my big media job altogether, we sought refuge at the South Carolina home. We needed a breather as a family. A restart, of sorts. Factor in COVID-19 and the subsequent quarantine, an extended vacation to our lake property was a no-brainer.

We thought we'd only be in South Carolina for a few weeks, so we'd packed only a few outfit changes. I still laugh about the time I asked John to bring back some clothes for me on one of his trips back to New York, where our New York life was packed up in a few PODS. Um, he did, all right. He brought back two wool skirts, two bikinis, and a pair of leather pants. It was June and approximately 5,987 degrees in the South. When I asked him about what he chose, he replied, "You weren't specific."

Apparently, our ideas of essentials diverge. And packing up a family of five by himself was not on John's bucket list. Thank God for Walmart and Target, the sources of my entire wardrobe for 2020.

To be honest, moving to South Carolina was a pretty difficult decision. I was truly struggling with leaving my full-time career in journalism. I'm not the type to run away from my problems, but uprooting our entire family was really the only choice. Without my income, a New York City lifestyle was out of the question.

You know the saying, "You can take the girl out of the newsroom, but you can't take the newsroom out of the girl?" No? Well, I am the embodiment of that truism. After we accepted the fact that we moved from a city of eight million to a town of just under three thousand, everyone around me resumed life-as-normal. Everyone but me.

John continued working remotely at his New York City–based commercial real estate firm. My oldest son, JJ; daughter, Caroline; and youngest son, Landon (Land-o) didn't skip a beat when the school year started back in person that fall of 2020. They quickly connected to friends through sports and class—for which I am incredibly grateful.

But I had an itch. I'm a challenger and a disrupter by nature. When I learned of the experiences of the millions of women who lost their jobs at the beginning of the pandemic, I knew I had to hear their stories.

And do you want to know what I uncovered? A similar narrative was echoed in the lives of every working mother I talked to—maybe not down to the minutiae, but in the way being a working mom makes us feel. We're all experiencing the same feelings of desperate burnout, the barbaric conflict of mom guilt, and bone-weary exhaustion of carrying it all. We're all feeling like we're failing everywhere—at work and at home. And to add insult to injury, most of us are underpaid while we're doing it.

God forbid we ever leave the workforce to focus on our family. Good luck explaining that eight-year resume gap to your next potential boss. According to a recent study, women who take time to stay home with children are often perceived as less capable and are less likely to be hired or promoted, while fathers are perceived as more capable.[3] (Don't get me started.)

Then there are the moms who are trying to work and parent. They pay exorbitant childcare fees to drop off and pick up their kids while it's still dark outside—burning the candle on both ends while spending up to 50 percent of their paycheck in the process.[4] Because—this just in—the cost of childcare has risen 70 percent since 1960, while wages have barely grown to assuage the sting.[5]

It is now more expensive to put your kid in daycare for a year than it is to pay in-state college tuition. Let that sink in.

Between 1962 and 2000, women's labor force participation increased from 37 percent to 61 percent, leading to an estimated $2 trillion in economic gains.[6] But women's workforce participation began to decline between 2000 and 2016, dipping from 60.7 percent to 57.2 percent. At least one study suggests that the rising cost of childcare has driven many women back to being stay-at-home moms—even when they'd rather be working outside the home.[7]

Cue the pandemic.

Millions of workers were forced from jobs in 2020 as businesses around the world closed their doors during the public health crisis. Women account for approximately 2 million of those lost jobs. But as the world reopened from February 2021 to January 2022, men regained the jobs they had lost due to COVID-19.[8] That was not the case for women, though. Here's the kicker: Women were still down by 1.6 million jobs during that same time period. Quick math: Barely 25 percent of women who lost their jobs went back to work.[9]

Because we're out-earned by our male counterparts by around 18 percent[10] (that number is even more egregious if you compare what mothers make compared to fathers; it's closer to 30 percent less), it just "makes sense" that we are the ones to stay home and care for the children. Right?

THE HAPPY GAP

The more mothers I spoke with, the more research I did, the more experts I spoke with, and the more books I read, the more I realized that we have an alarming problem in our country. And, yes, it is an *American* problem. Mom guilt doesn't really exist elsewhere to the extent it does here in the US. In fact, the US has the most disparate "happy gap" between parents and non-parents.[11]

> Mom guilt doesn't really exist elsewhere to the extent it does here in the US.

When I read this statistic, I knew I had to know more. I

reached out to researcher Jennifer Glass, a sociology professor at the University of Texas and the executive director of the Council on Contemporary Families. I asked her what a "happy gap" even meant. Here's what she said: "I was doing a bit of innovative research for the *American Journal of Sociology* back in 2016. I learned that the happy gap between non-parents and parents is the largest in the United States. We stand out because of this gap—it's *tiny* in other countries. In America, parents report being 12 percent less happy than non-parents."[12]

Wow. Isn't that sad?

According to Glass, our happy gap is closely associated with the stress and strain of raising kids in our country. Our social policies are simply not geared toward supporting parents and working families. For example, collective group care is well supported in Europe. They raise children as a collective responsibility, a community. Early childhood systems are integrated into education so that the cognitive development of children isn't solely left up to their parents. This early childhood development starts as early as two years old in France and three years old in the United Kingdom, and it's seen as schooling. Over half of the stay-at-home moms in those countries send their kids to preschool.

When Glass first saw this gap, it proved everything she'd been researching. It was a smoking gun. Prior to Glass's research, the idea that parenting really *doesn't* make us happier people hadn't really been discussed—at least not publicly.

The "happy gap" is an American phenomenon. "I had no idea that the happiness gap didn't really exist elsewhere," Glass explained to me. "The truth is, we do a lousy job of supporting families and parents in our country. In other countries, there is a community-based responsibility to raise children. They are their 'brother's keeper.' That is not at all how American society views child-rearing."

You don't say? I'm sure we *all* could have come to the same conclusion. But isn't it refreshing to have a PhD back us up? It's not just a feeling. It's a fact.

BEING A WORKING MOM IN AMERICA IS HARDER THAN IT'S EVER BEEN

The tension you're feeling as you're reading these statistics is the same fuel that led me to create CARRY Media, which exists to celebrate, champion, and advocate for the working mom through disruptive storytelling, content, and resources. We think that being a working mom should work, and we aim to beat the drum, blaze the trails, and tell the story of what it's like to be a working mom in America so we can enact change.

Now, we're not out to burn bras or bridges. This book isn't an anti-male manifesto. Not at all. In fact, we need men on our journey to equitable, fair dynamics at home and in the workplace. We need men on our team. Why? *Because we need men in this fight.* I'm a proud #boymom of two sons that I love with my whole heart.

This is *not* a case against men. This is a case *for* moms on their workplace journey.

This also isn't a commentary on traditional gender roles. While we will trace how gender roles have changed and shifted over the history of our country, we will only do so to help further our understanding of how women went from being medieval beer brewers who worked shoulder to shoulder with their husbands to the burned-out, exhausted, carry-it-all martyrs of working motherhood we are today.

I'll never forget when I returned to work after having Caroline, my first baby. I had been shopping just days before to find camera-appropriate outfits to put on my strange new body. If you've carried a child before, you know what body I'm talking about. The one that feels *tiny* after months of growing a human being, but then you put on your pre-pregnancy jeans and realize that you still have a long, long way to go before that button is reaching its hole.

In searching for my postpartum wardrobe (and I mean *searching*, because the good stores are few and far between), I was quickly annoyed by the "bounce-back shapewear" messages I kept encountering. They felt demeaning. They felt demanding. The only things I had bouncing back were the huge, milk-filled boobs that had taken over the top half of my body. Or maybe the extra ten pounds I was carrying in my face and neck. Or could it have been the saddlebags that cropped up on my thighs out of nowhere? I was bouncing, all right. I just don't think it was in the way the ads were screaming I should be.

I felt like an alien inside my own skin.

So, there I was, weepy over leaving my baby, boobs swollen and aching to be pumped, shoved into a pair of pants that were squeezing me like a sausage casing. I walked into the newsroom and my male coworker looked up.

"Hey, Paula," he said cheerily. "How was your vacation?"

Before you ask, no, he wasn't being sarcastic.

I've covered my fair share of news stories where women snap and have unthinkable, violent reactions that don't make sense after the fact. In that moment, with his well-rested eyes, clothes with zero signs of crusty spit-up, and cup of *hot* coffee, I almost became one of those women.

"My…vacation?" I repeated. Surely he was joking.

He didn't pick up on my incredulity. "Six weeks without a newsroom wake-up call? That sounds like a vacation to me!"

I wanted to tell him about the "I'm hungry" wake-up calls. The "I want to use you as a human pacifier" wake-up calls. The "I'm wet or dirty or both" wake-up calls. The "I enjoy the sound of my own screams" wake-up calls my luxurious "vacation" had afforded me. Or how about my own wake-up calls? The "is that more discharge or am I that sweaty" wake-up calls. The "my boobs are about to explode" wake-up calls. Or every new mother's favorite, the "let's imagine every horrible possibility about my child" wake-up calls.

So I said, "My nipples are on fire from nursing, I haven't slept for more than four consecutive hours in two months, and my vagina is still healing from the severe tearing I had during giving birth. My vacation was awesome. Thanks for asking."

He felt horrible. Truly, he was at a loss for words. It was like he had no idea what *actually* happens when a human exits a woman's body. Maybe he didn't. I feel that a bit of that responsibility lies on us—women.

We go through the arduous and less than lovely process of labor and delivery, and the next photo you see is of us in a hospital bed, tucked beneath crisp white sheets with coiffed hair, mascara, and a baby burrito swaddled in our arms.

Look, I get that we don't want to post photos of our two-in-the-morning feedings, bleary-eyed and barely human as the nurses and techs barge in and out of the dark room repeatedly the very moment our eyes get heavy enough to close and bless us with the respite of a few seconds of sleep. We don't want to show the world what's tucked beneath the seventeen scratchy blankets in our photos—and that's okay. The mesh underwear, soggy pads, and healing incisions don't make for palatable social media content.

But what if we talked about it more? And not just whispered behind curved hands at the nail salon. What if we talked about what it's like to bring a child into this world openly and publicly? I don't know about you, but I was unpleasantly surprised when I returned home from the hospital with Caroline. No baby book or girlfriend warned me of the weeks of bleeding I'd experience. Or the way my uterus contracting would bring actual tears of acute pain to my eyes. Or about that first post-delivery poop.

I left my coworker slack-jawed and speechless, and I went to my cubicle. I sat in the chair and cried my tired eyes out. Maybe it wasn't the first time I'd been unguarded when a man made a ridiculous statement about being a working woman, but it was the first time I could remember feeling defeated by it.

Every time I've avoided gently (or not so gently) educating a male coworker just to keep the peace or fit in, or simply because I was too tired in the moment, I've failed myself. And I've failed you too.

A Rock Star Employee

Women, we must own our stories. We must own our worth and value. We're not martyrs. We're not weak. We're not less than. We're sort of superhumans. Seriously—we grow people. We perpetuate the human race. Instead of isolating ourselves in this fight, let's *invite* men into the conversation by having rational, honest, and two-sided conversations about ourselves, our thoughts, and our journeys. They don't know what they don't know. And part of that is on us.

That's why I've made it my ultimate goal to remind the

American workforce that moms not only deserve a seat at the table, but that businesses *need* moms to have a seat at the table. We bring an intrinsic, immeasurable value.

The mission for CARRY Media is simple:

- To make sure a mom's voice is valued in the workforce and motherhood is celebrated, instead of scrutinized.
- To make sure that being a mom isn't viewed by the workforce as a risk, liability, or weakness.
- To make sure moms have a choice whether or not we want to work.

I saw a quote the other day: "If you want to get shit done, hire a woman. If you want to get *everything* done, hire a mother." Isn't that the truth? Is there a more skilled multitasker than a working mom?

We are the most resourceful, most reliable, most caring candidates a company could hire. Which raises the obvious question:

Why aren't they?

Why doesn't corporate America value working mothers? In fact, why aren't they actively recruiting working moms to fortify their companies? Amy Henderson is the CEO of TendLab, a business she built to transform our culture's relationship to parenthood. In her research to understand the complexities of modern parenthood, Amy found that "80% of all parents…reported developing an enhanced capacity in many core areas: emotional intelligence, courage, purpose, efficiency, productivity, and the ability to collaborate."[13]

Sounds like a rock star employee to me. That's a person I want on my team. That's a person I *need* on my team.

So why aren't companies chasing us down and offering top dollar, flexibility, and anything else we need to work for them? It's a statistical fact that companies with more women executives are more likely to outperform those with fewer senior women.[14] So what's the deal?

And if American companies *do* value working mothers, why is it next to impossible to be a working mom and *not* feel like you're failing on all fronts? Why is it so difficult to strike the right balance? To live out our passions as both mothers and workers? Why is being a working mom in America so dang hard?

I have had the pleasure of interviewing many mothers in a myriad of professional fields. From the president and owner of In-N-Out Burger, Lynsi Snyder, to the mom sitting next to me at the travel volleyball tournament with a side hustle. One delightful conversation I had was interviewing my friend Jenna Bush Hager on my *Faith & Calling* podcast, which I launched out of a closet in my South Carolina home during the pandemic. She shared a story with me that I think is a microcosm of the working mom experience in America. She said that when she was pregnant with her third baby, she was in the middle of a promotion at NBC News. Kathie Lee Gifford was stepping away from *Kathie Lee and Hoda*, and Jenna was being considered as her replacement.

There was a point in the process when Jenna suspected she was pregnant. She did the math, and the birth of her third child, Hal, would coincide with the start date for the new show. Jenna was hesitant to share her news. "Nobody ever once said, 'Oh no, you're going to have to go on maternity leave,'" Jenna said. "But I couldn't believe that it was the year 2019 and this [fear] was something we were still experiencing."

Jenna's husband had also recently started a new job at the time of the pregnancy. "And yet, he would never have worried about bringing another child into the world," said Jenna, explaining how women experience an "internal fear" about how our pregnancies will affect our careers. "Nobody made me feel one ounce of guilt or shame or worry," Jenna said, "but I think as women, we are programmed to worry."

My interviews with Jenna left me wrestling with some heavy questions.

If the daughter of a former United States president is hesitant to share what *should be* the most exciting news of her life for fear of losing out on an opportunity at work, how much *more* is the everyday working mom conflicted regarding her own pregnancy? Regarding motherhood?

Why is the greatest gift we have as women, the gift of being capable of creating life, regarded as something women should feel ashamed of? I mean, it's like a super-power. A woman's body can build a human brain. Toes. Eyeballs. Hearts. A woman's body can do what a man's can't. And yet this sacred and miraculous ability is not celebrated. Instead, working moms are punished for it.

> Why is the greatest gift we have as women, the gift of being capable of creating life, regarded as something women should feel ashamed of?

It's stories like Jenna's that make it abundantly clear that culture and corporations need to do better by working moms. *All* working moms. We'll get specific too. We'll ask questions like, why are female CEOs more likely to be fired than male CEOs? Why won't the salary gap be closed until 2059? Why is senior management 71 percent male even though companies with more women executives are more likely to outperform those with fewer women? One suggestion that might eliminate *all* of those disparities? We need more women at the table. We need more women in decision-making roles. And then *we*—the women—need to speak up. On our own behalf and others'.

A BETTER WAY FORWARD

I mentioned that after moving to South Carolina, my midlife crisis included buying a Jeep Wrangler. But this wasn't just any Jeep. I wanted to get it lifted. When the salesman asked how high, I said, "I want to pull my groin getting in and out of it." Mission accomplished.

In some ways, this book you're holding or listening to is an example of my lifted Jeep.

When I was tasked with doing some research on how we could improve our corporate culture for working moms while at ABC News, I embarked on a journey of discovery that continues to this day. What started off as a fourteen-page document has now become the book you're holding. Together, we are going to do a bit of fascinating research. We're going to look at where we went wrong as a country. Spoiler alert: You are *not* going to be happy with the 1950s moms in our nation's history. Dangit, June Cleaver.

We're going to look at companies that are getting it right—and there are many who are. We're going to see what their practices look like and make some practical suggestions for how other companies can work toward similar standards.

We're going to hear stories from working moms all over the world. You may be shocked (or not) to hear that the American mother is at a far greater disadvantage than mothers in some countries you may consider to be less developed or less progressive.

There's *so much* at stake here. Amy Henderson of TendLab describes the importance of finding ways corporate America can support mothers and our families: "How parents are treated and held and protected and supported is the greatest reflection of a nation. Because how we parent is the foundation of everything: what we value, what we stand for, who we are, and who we're becoming."[15] The need is real. And the need is urgent.

But most of all, above and beyond the statistics and data and stories, if you get nothing else from this book, I hope that you hear this: You don't have to carry it all. We know you can, at least for a while. Heck, you can carry a preschooler on one hip and an entire week's worth of grocery bags on the other. And the random toy your kid hands you, thinking you've got capacity for one more thing.

But you weren't created to carry it all. There is a better way forward—a way that we're going to discover together. The problems we have as a country and culture are not insurmountable. Besides, we've got moms on this job. And there are literally no hands more capable than hers.

CHAPTER TWO

CARRYING ON THE TRADITION

I wish I could be two people at the same time and experience both fully. I absolutely love time with my kids, but I am aware of all the emails that are piling up for me. I try to give myself grace and remind myself that I am doing the best I can.

—Anna Malaika Tubbs, mom of two, author

One of the biggest misconceptions about working in network TV is that it's all glitz and glamour all the time.

"You get to interview famous celebrities! You get to travel to exotic locations! You get to cover the most exciting stories!"

Well, yes. But there are a lot of behind-the-scenes stories that I'm extremely thankful never made it to air. Take the first time I met Bradley Cooper, for instance.

Before *Good Morning America* one morning, I was walking out of the bathrooms and—wouldn't you know it?—there was Bradley Cooper. You know, the Grammy Award–winning, Academy Award–nominated *(nine times!)*, Golden Globe–nominated, Tony Award–nominated, and completely gorgeous Bradley Cooper. That one.

His dressing room was located directly across the hall from the women's restroom, and for some reason, Bradley happened to be standing in his doorway. We made eye contact, and not wanting to be rude, I walked over to introduce myself. Only the bathroom had been out of paper towels, so my hands were still wet.

"Sorry," I said as I offered him a damp handshake. "No paper towels in the bathroom."

And those, dear friends, were my first words to Bradley Freaking Cooper. Of note, my hair was also pinned up in a menagerie of Velcro curlers *and* I was every minute of thirty-eight weeks pregnant.

Not at all how I pictured that introduction. (Sidebar: He was a super nice guy and did nothing to magnify the awkwardness of the situation. I did that *all* on my own.)

Another bathroom incident comes to mind, this one involving the queen herself, Dolly Parton.

GIRLS THAT PEE TOGETHER
STAY TOGETHER

Once again, as a mother of three, I had to use the bathroom before anchoring *GMA*. I walked inside and found the right stall was ajar. Because my body gives me about three seconds' notice before it starts to pee, with or without a toilet present, I was in a rush. I pushed open the door to find Dolly Parton *staring me in the face*. To be more accurate, I hit the queen with the bathroom door.

I took two steps back until I ran into the wall. All I could say was, "Oh my gosh, it's Dolly Parton."

Yes. My wit in these situations astounds me as well.

I realized my mistake the very moment our eyes met: That stall's door didn't lock. Luckily, she had already finished taking care of business and was already buttoned up and standing, ready to walk out. My brain wouldn't work. I couldn't force out another word. I'd never experienced such humiliation juxtaposed with jaw-dropping awe before. I mean—it was Dolly! Like seeing a mythical creature up close. A unicorn in the bathroom.

Finally, I began apologizing profusely. Dolly, unsurprisingly, couldn't have been sweeter.

"It's okay, sweetie," she said. "I do my best work in the bathroom."

I couldn't have worshipped her more. Then, later, when I bumped into her again just outside the studio, she said, "Girls that pee together stay together."

I have learned many meaningful lessons from Dolly, some of which I discussed in my last book, *Called Out*. But there's one lesson from Dolly I think we all can learn from, a difficult lesson that reveals an even more difficult reality for working mothers.

I read an interview with Dolly where she was asked about her and her longtime love and husband, Carl Dean, never having children. Here's how the interview read:

"Yeah," [Dolly] says. She seems to have a clear picture of them, these kids that didn't come. "You always wonder," she says. "My husband and I, when we first got married, we thought about if we had kids, what would they look like? Would they be tall—because he's tall? Or would they be little squats like me? If we'd had a girl, she was gonna be called Carla…Anyway, we talked about it, and we dreamed it, but it wasn't meant to be. Now that we're older? We're glad."

Why? "I would have been a great mother, I think. I would probably have given up everything else. Because I would've felt guilty about that, if I'd have left them [to work, to tour]. Everything would have changed. I probably wouldn't have been a star."[1]

Before I unpack Dolly's comments, I want to be clear: *I do not believe you have to be a mother to be fulfilled as a woman.* In fact, it's my understanding that Dolly has no regrets about the choices she's made or the choices life made for her. She's a benevolent and generous philanthropist and has done immeasurable good for children in need, not the least of which is her foundation Imagination Library, a nonprofit that provides free books to preschoolers.

Dolly said in another interview, "If I had it to do it all over, I'd do it all over again."[2]

What I *do* want to draw attention to is the underlying message of Dolly's reaction to not having kids of her own: *Everything would have changed. I probably wouldn't have been a star.* Somewhere along the way, Dolly either noticed or learned that being a mother in America limits you. It creates a ceiling you cannot schedule, manipulate, or power around. No matter how much money or influence you have, being a working mom doesn't work.

Why don't men experience this same ceiling? Aren't they equally responsible for the children that serve as a roadblock for women? And why are kids and taking care of them viewed as roadblocks?

Why doesn't the term *working father* have a place in our vernacular? Why isn't everybody talking about *dad guilt*?

I was having a conversation with an acquaintance named Beth, and she asked me a startling question: "Has America always hated women?" I had to pause the conversation. I hadn't even been talking about my book or anything related to the idea of women in the workplace. I was caught off guard.

"Talk more about that," I said.

Beth is from Toronto, Canada. She's been in the United States for the last seven years working as an executive coach. Beth said, "In Canada, when I'd walk into a boardroom, there was almost always equal representation between women and men. But in America, when I walk into a boardroom, it's almost always *exclusively* men. Why is that?"

Great question, Beth. You've come to the right place.

In the last chapter, we touched briefly on some data surrounding the disparity between working fathers and working mothers and how they are treated and acknowledged in the workplace. I don't know if you finished needing to fan the flames of rage that arose in your belly, but I want to warn you: It's going to get worse before it gets better.

I want this book to be something that sparks hope and intentional action. Change is possible—in fact, it's already happening! But to get to our solutions, we've got to confront some cold, hard facts about the problems.

> Change is possible—in fact, it's already happening!

Let's start at the beginning—the beginning of a relationship, that is. Before the babies are made.

CARRYING CARE

When I met John, we were at a conservative Christian college in Ohio, and I was two years ahead of him. The joke on campus was that the girls were there to get their "MRS" degree. In fact, some of my friends and I dressed up like pregnant MRS candidates for Halloween. I guess you could say I've never been afraid to challenge the status quo.

But in all seriousness, almost all my friends got married young. I was one of the last to get married—at the ripe old age of twenty-four. I was in roughly thirteen weddings before my own.

John and I started dating in 1996, very casually at first. It was my senior year, and I was so sick of everyone assuming I wanted to find a husband. In reality, I just wanted to hang out with someone fun and have a good time. So, to prove my point, I set my sights on John, a sophomore. Nothing serious, right?

I was on the verge of getting my degree in broadcast communications and set to embark on an internship at CNN/SI in Atlanta just a few months later. We dated casually for a bit, then when I graduated, I realized there was something more. John agreed, and we ended up getting married in 2000.

I always carried this tension: I wanted to work, but felt conflicted in reconciling my wiring to the traditional roles I'd grown up with in church and in my home.

When we were first married, I was selling airtime on a Columbus, Ohio, radio station. I was making a pretty dang good living too. Then, September 11 happened. Something inside me shifted. A fire inside me had been lit—I wanted to bring the news into American homes.

That dream that others had seen for me—including my college professors and John—was one I finally saw for myself. I was ready to press into my fears and insecurities to chase the TV thing.

So, what did I do? I quit my lucrative radio sales job and handed out my resume to all the local stations in Dayton, Ohio. Only one bit. Ian Rubin, the news director at WKEF/WRGT-TV, gave me a shot at being a production assistant for *seven bucks an hour*.

Five years into marriage, John was coaching college basketball at Central State University, an HBCU (historically Black college or university)—coaching was his dream job. John's always been my biggest encourager, often believing in me more than I believed in myself. So a few years later, when I got the opportunity to work at the NBC affiliate in Chicago—the third-largest TV market in America—John put his dreams on hold to come with me and pursue mine.

Bottom line: I wouldn't have made it to the pinnacle of broadcasting without the support of my husband.

> My story of spousal equality is the exception, even among the practices of the most brilliant minds in our country.

But here's what I also know: My story of spousal equality is the exception, even among the practices of the most brilliant minds in our country.

THE "MOM DEFAULT"

A 2014 study of more than twenty-five thousand Harvard Business School graduates revealed that both men and women value fulfilling professional *and* personal lives, but the means by which they realize their goals played out differently according to gender.[3]

Here's the gist of the findings: More than half the men surveyed said that when they left Harvard Business School, they expected that their careers would take priority over their spouse's or partner's. Eighty-three percent of these men reported being married. Of note, this expectation was less prevalent among men of color. For men of color, 48 percent anticipated that their spouse's career would be of equal importance to their own, compared to 39 percent of white men.

While a little more than half of the men graduating from Harvard Business School expected their careers to take precedence over their spouses', close to 75 percent reported in a follow-up survey that their jobs actually *did* become the priority in the marriage.

This is where our problem originates. There's a reason this idea that women should carry most of the child-rearing exists and persists, and we'll get into that history in the next chapter. But right now, let's consider the modern-day effects of treating women as the default care providers.

You get married. You both want to have success in your careers and family. Then the first baby comes home from the hospital, and what happens? In most cases, the husband goes back to work fairly quickly, leaving the mom to figure out schedules, childcare, and a new distribution of responsibilities.

Why? Because her body is capable of creating food for her baby? Is that God's or evolution's way of telling us that the mother should be the primary caregiver? If that's your argument, you could also reason that a man's superior physical strength is a similar indicator that *he* should provide the majority of care, seeing as how he is capable of protecting and defending his young.

If you ask me, a physiological analysis of our bodies only serves to prove that men and women are *both* built to care for their children equally. The "mom default" is not intuitive, nor is it effective in a culture where the majority of families require dual incomes to survive.

> The "mom default" is not intuitive, nor is it effective in a culture where the majority of families require dual incomes to survive.

For us to think the "traditional" mindset of dads heading to the office while Mom stays behind in the kitchen isn't limiting working mothers would be to ignore the obvious truth. In my research, I've learned that the "traditional" family model simply doesn't work...or really even exist. We're going to dive deep into this soon.

These expectations don't exist in a corner or in the shadows of our nation. It's happening to women graduating from Harvard Business School, to middle-class mothers, and to those who are the most underresourced in our country. This mom guilt tension is felt by every working mother that I've spoken with in every corner of our country—some more than others, but it's certainly present with all.

When American women *do* return to work, it's almost always too early. A medically reviewed article posted by Medicine.net reports that it takes six months to a year for your body to heal after giving birth.[4] I personally know zero American mothers who were offered or took a six-month maternity leave. I certainly didn't. I was still wearing pads and pumping in bathrooms when I got back to filing stories and filming segments. Why?

Fear.

Restlessness.

It was the norm.

I didn't know any better.

I cobbled together vacation and sick time to stretch out my maternity leave with Landon to about twelve weeks. I had Land-o on January 7. Twelve weeks later, my first day back at work was April Fool's Day.

God has a sense of humor.

I had been cleared to work, but not to work out. I was barely cleared to do the thing that got me pregnant in the first place. And yet the expectations to appear as if I'd never been pregnant at all were there.

When I returned to *Good Morning America* to file my first report postpartum, one of the network executives sent me an email about my "look."

"Not your best look," it read.

You don't say.

I knew I wasn't at my best. I still had the baby weight. Because, you know, my body is healthy and normal and had pushed out a human fewer than ninety days prior. I also still had my pregnancy mask—a gift from Landon to me, better known as melasma. I was exhausted. My hormones were raging. And I had never felt more vulnerable in my entire life.

Here I was, having just furthered society, already feeling doughy and scrutinized. I don't get *one day* under my belt before an executive is picking apart the way I look?

I responded back: *Just had a baby. First day back from leave. Already don't feel great about myself. If you could give me some grace, I'd appreciate it.*

I cried. And then I got angry.

It wasn't because I was an amateur. This was my third kid. I'd been there twice before. I felt so vulnerable because I knew what was ahead for me as a working mother. I knew what I was up against, now times *three*.

What I should have said back was, *Oh, you mean the Teflon tights I have pulled up to my bra line to smooth out the dimples of my ravaged stomach? How terrible for you that you noticed. Meanwhile, I can't fully inhale.*

My hair was done. I had makeup on. I was wearing clothes that matched. No, they weren't designer postpartum duds, but that's not my style. In my opinion, "transitional" clothing that I'll wear for two months is not a wise financial investment. It's almost like we're expected to "bounce back" to the exact same size. Which is absolutely bananas. I've seen plenty of articles from reputable news outlets as well as social media posts reinforcing the ridiculous expectation that the quicker we can look as if we've never just created a human, the better.

With a newborn and two other littles at home, the fact that I was able to string together news copy was a miracle. This executive should have been praising my return to work, not criticizing my appearance.

Weeks after the executive's comments, I was asked to travel to Brazil to cover soccer's World Cup in Rio. Landon was still an infant and I was nursing, and I didn't want to be a country away from him. So I decided to take him with me. The only issue was the same issue that beleaguers working moms of all socioeconomic statuses across the country: childcare. Who would keep Landon while I was working?

This was an incredible assignment to be asked to cover. I didn't want to miss out on the opportunity, because who knew when I'd get the chance to cover an event that big again.

I was put in touch with a Rio-based nanny through a friend. When Landon and I arrived, it was the first time I laid eyes on her. Don't get me wrong—she was precious and kind and wonderful. But we spoke very few words of the same language, and it suddenly dawned on me that I was about to leave one of my most valuable possessions, my *baby*, with a complete stranger.

Not to mention the political climate in the city. Prior to the first kickoff, anti–World Cup protesters flooded the streets in demonstration against the "high cost of stadiums, corruption, police brutality and evictions."[5] These weren't silent protests, either. Protesters started fires, threw rocks, and were allegedly responsible for an aggressive police response that led to a CNN anchor's broken arm.

Only slightly less intense than the riots was my experience pumping breastmilk in a foreign country, which is about as fun as it sounds—miserable. After a particularly arduous day, I hadn't pumped in nearly ten hours, and I was in a ton of pain. My boobs felt like they were going to explode. It was during the US Men's National Team's elimination game—in other words, I had to be at the stadium for the entire day.

I got in the car to head to the airport with my producer, Emily Stanitz. It was literally the first time we'd worked together. I apologized and then said, "I have to pump." Like, now. In the back seat. We got to know one another very quickly through that experience.

Why did I put myself through so much torture? Because I was terrified to turn down an assignment. I bet you've said yes to similar torture. Because this is how women get ahead. We show we can carry it all. And we'll kill ourselves (or, at a bare minimum, risk mastitis) to do it.

> We say yes as working mothers to the most ridiculous standards and practices because if we say no, we are put in time out.

We say yes as working mothers to the most ridiculous standards and practices because if we say no, we are put in time out. We aren't "team players" anymore. In fact, we're a problem. A risk. A ticking time bomb. We feel our days are numbered.

NEWS OF INEQUITIES

I could give countless examples of the incongruent treatment between men and women in network television. I was told by a male superior early in my career that I'd never make it on TV unless I showed my boobs. Only *boobs* was not the word he used. He also "helpfully" informed me that women had no place in sports news. No, this wasn't the 1960s. This was in the 2000s.

After I left that station, I reported my experience. To my knowledge, nothing was ever done about it. But I know I'm not the only one with stories like these. Others have stories with even grimier and more demeaning details. As far as women have advanced over the last few decades, it's still very much a "boys' club" at many organizations and businesses.

In the world of network news, a male anchor pretty much gets to wear whatever he wants. But as a female anchor, your outfit has to be "approved" before you go on air.

When I was covering election night 2016 for ABC News in Florida, I received the following text: "Need you to put on grown up shoes and no leggings. If you have fancy TV shoes, please put them on, and if not, ask them to shoot you tight."

What was I wearing? A green silk top and dark pants from Rag

& Bone with black slip-ons. Just for context, I was preparing to work around the clock. I brought my pillow to our live location at the University of Miami. We were prepared for voting to go well into the night and to stay live throughout the night as well. Some of my male counterparts were wearing blue jeans. Did they get a text? Of course not. Oh, and for the record, they too thought the double standard was ridiculous.

There are countless similar incidents. Like the time I was asked to put on more foundation because my "pregnancy mask" was showing. Or how all the female correspondents were sent to a recommended stylist upon hire. There, we were told what we had to look like and what we had to wear—and then we had to pay for it. We weren't given a stipend. Think that happened with our male counterparts? I can't recall a single similar incident.

If you've seen *The Morning Show* with Jennifer Aniston and Reese Witherspoon, you've seen a fairly accurate (albeit exaggerated) picture of what it's like to be a female journalist and news anchor. In preparation for her role, Jennifer Aniston stopped by the *Good Morning America* set in Times Square.

Miraculously, there were no bathroom-related incidents connected to her visit. But I was a little starstruck talking to Rachel—um, I mean, *Jennifer*—up close and personal. No cameras. Just chatting.

We talked casually in the control room for over half an hour about what it was like to be a woman in network television. I told her the truth: So much of it comes down to our appearance. And not just whether or not we looked polished and professional, but whether or not we wore the same dress too close together in our wardrobe rotation.

You're going to love this story.

There's an Australian news anchor named Karl Stefanovic who wore the same suit every day for an entire year…and *no one noticed*. It was an experiment he did in response to the ridiculous amount of criticism female co-anchors received that he never experienced as a man.

Karl was quoted in the *Sydney Morning Herald* as saying, "I've worn the same suit on air for a year—except for a couple of times because of circumstance—to make a point. "I'm judged on my interviews, my appalling sense of humour—on how I do my job, basically. Whereas women are quite often judged on what they're wearing or how their hair is…that's [what I wanted to test]."[6]

Karl is friends with Samantha Armytage, the co-host of a rival news show. The *Herald* article said, "Earlier this year, News Corp tabloid *The Daily Telegraph* dredged up old photographs of Armytage running errands in comfortable clothes, then published them because…well, the purpose of the story was never entirely clear."

Karl said, "She's a mate and she was hurt by that…And I can understand. You've got to have a thick skin in TV, but there's a limit."

He says, "No one has noticed [my suit]; no one gives a shit… But women, they wear the wrong color and they get pulled up. They say the wrong thing and there's thousands of tweets written about them. Women are judged much more harshly and keenly for what they do, what they say and what they wear."

Karl, I don't know you. But I love you for this.

Like Karl's friend and fellow TV anchor Samantha, I didn't get into journalism because I was into fashion. I didn't get into journalism because I had beauty pageant aspirations. In fact, no one who knows me well would accuse me of caring much about what I wear at all. At home, give me a Michigan sweatshirt and pair of leggings. I might change into jeans if we go out to dinner. Emphasis on *I might*. Left to my own devices at *GMA*, where I bought my own clothes, you'd regularly find me on air in a fifty-dollar Marshalls special.

But when I was asked to do *The View*, they bought our clothes for us. The lead wardrobe stylist took me to Saks and told me I could have anything I wanted for the show. It was such an out-of-body experience. On-air staff are loaned many of the clothes and have an arrangement to buy some of them.

Anyway, I'm not a fancy gal. I had boxed wine at my wedding. I went to Buffalo Wild Wings with my husband for my 40th birthday. When I treat myself, it's usually by grabbing a ninety-nine-cent fountain drink from the gas station.

You get it.

The stylist bought me several pairs of Manolo Blahnik shoes, which are a very high-end brand. But I continued to call them Milano Blahnik shoes. Milano, like the cookies. My producer, Katie den Daas, couldn't take it anymore. She bought me a package of Milano cookies and wrote a note saying, "These are the cookies, those are the shoes." I finally understood (and I've never been able to look at Milano cookies the same...thank you, Katie xo).

All that to say, fashion isn't my lane. It never will be. I can't dress myself or my house. I have no interest in it. I admire those who do. But I didn't get into journalism for the free shoes. I got into journalism because I love asking questions and telling people's stories. My nickname growing up was Paula Twenty Questions. It's the same reason (I assume) men get into journalism. And yet we're consistently and systematically judged and held to completely different standards.

The gender pay gap I experienced doesn't just exist in network television. It's *everywhere*, from fast food workers to conglomerate CEOs. Women, on average, earn less income than men serving in similar positions.

Yes, there has been a significant uptick in the number of public conversations regarding the gender pay gap, but that hasn't really affected the bottom line. While it may *appear* that a woman's career opportunities are limitless today, that's simply not what the data tells us. According to a *Harvard Business Review* article, "Women make up about half of all college-educated workers in the United States, and they hold jobs in virtually every industry, working in more than 300 occupations tracked by the federal government. Yet women remain underrepresented in positions of power, often drastically so: Just 8% of *Fortune* 500 companies are led by women, and less than 1% by women of color."[7]

That gap narrows a bit in professional service firms, where 20 percent of CEOs are women. And despite trending conversations and suggested legislation to increase the number of women sitting on boards, women hold fewer than 20 percent of those seats at Fortune 500 companies—which is sadly still an improvement when compared to years past.

In the same study of 25,000 Harvard Business School graduates we discussed earlier, an overwhelming 77 percent of those surveyed say that they believe that "prioritizing family over work" was the number one barrier to women's career advancement. "As one alumna in her mid-thirties noted, a key factor is still 'deep-rooted attitudes that a woman should be the primary caregiver, so it is "understood" that her career may have to take a backseat for a while as similar male colleagues move ahead at a more rapid pace.'"[8]

The gap between men's and women's advancement to senior

positions has not changed, despite an increase in the number of women who are credentialed and experienced enough to assume top roles. It's not that the talent isn't there; it's that the talent isn't valued. More often than not, women are offered only roles with limited mobility and aren't groomed for executive leadership. Why?

Probably because she may do something crazy like perpetuate the human race with a pesky pregnancy. I know. *What* is she thinking?

DOUBLE STANDARDS

Let's say a woman does overcome the statistical odds and becomes the CEO of a company, a board member, or some other part of senior management. It's all equal then, right? Because she's doing the exact same job at the exact same level as her male counterpart?

Not at all.

My TV agent and I were eating lunch one afternoon. I had just resigned from a position, and the topic of my replacement came up. They had chosen a man.

"What kind of contract did they extend to him?" I asked.

My agent looked me straight in the eye. "A good one."

"Better than mine?" *That can't be possible*, I thought. I'd been at that particular network for a while. My personal and professional investment there had been significant. I covered hundreds of stories and traveled all over the world. My replacement had no equity in the network. (Though, admittedly, he is a genuinely wonderful human.)

"Almost double," my agent said. This wasn't hearsay. We shared the same agency.

My male replacement was paid almost *double* my salary. It doesn't get a whole lot more offensive than that. But I remember reading somewhere that the pay gap between men and women was all but gone, that women and men were being fairly compensated. Isn't that what the Equal Pay Act of 1963 guarantees? Isn't it illegal to pay a man more money than a woman in the same role with similar experience?

It is, but it still happens.

In my conversations with other working moms and in my research, I found that I'm not the only woman experiencing pay discrimination. And network TV isn't the only sector.

So I did what I do: I kept digging. I learned that the pay gap is still hovering around a 16 percent differential, and that men are over three times more likely to be offered an executive role than women are.[9]

According to Pew Research Center, women earned 84 percent of what men earned in the year 2020.[10] To put it in simpler terms, a woman would have to work for free through February 11 of 2021 to earn the same salary as a man did by December 31, 2020—an extra forty-two days. (If that's not bad enough, it's even worse for moms. Mothers make 71 cents on the dollar compared to fathers, according to the American Association of University Women, an organization that measures the progress of women in the US.)[11]

> According to Pew Research Center, women earned 84 percent of what men earned in the year 2020.

In a study done by ExecThread that looked at 246 job opportunities presented by recruiters to their members for senior director, vice president, senior vice president, and C-suite positions, fifty-five of the job opportunities were presented to women, while 191 were presented to men.[12] (C-suite positions are any job titles with the letter *C* or word *chief* at the beginning: CEO, CFO, CMO. You get it.)

In the same study, they compared the average low- and high-end salary ranges of the job opportunities presented as well as the average midpoints of the compensation ranges. Any guesses what they found?

On average, men are presented with much higher-paying job opportunities than women.

On average, men are approached by executive recruiters for job opportunities that pay 12 percent more than those jobs that executive recruiters approached women for. One obvious reason the gender pay gap persists? Women aren't even offered the same jobs as men. We're not even given a chance. And if we do get a chance to peek over the glass ceiling, we're not even compensated for it. Another study done by Morningstar reported that the highest-paid senior women earned 81.5 cents compared to men in the same positions.[13] It's worth mentioning that women of color earn even less than that: 64 cents for black women and 57 cents for Latina women for every dollar earned by a white man.[14] And, once we get the job, we don't ask for raises nearly as much as men do.

Ladies, it's not enough to just know our worth. We must advocate for it. By the time you're done reading this book, you'll have all the tools you need to do just this.

> It's not enough to just know our worth. We must advocate for it.

BEAUTIFUL FRENCH COBBLESTONES

Indra Nooyi is a woman I look up to. In fact, I tried to get an interview with Indra for this book, but to no avail. (Indra! If you're reading this—call me! I am a fan.)

Indra was the CEO of PepsiCo from 2006 to 2018. Born in Chennai, India, Indra moved to the United States in 1978 to attend Yale University, after which she worked for various companies before joining PepsiCo as a senior vice president in 1994.

She told the 2019 Women in the World Summit that when she joined PepsiCo, her daughters were very young (a newborn and an eight-year-old)…If she couldn't go home and take care of the kids, "I decided that come…five o'clock, my kids were allowed to come to work and hang around. They were allowed to play; they were allowed to sleep in my office, do whatever."[15]

Were her bosses okay with it? Her response is epic: "Did they have a choice?…If you want me, that's the price of having me."

And, on the home front, she's said this about her husband: "And many times, it's the people around us—like our life partners—who make this juggling possible."[16]

Indra is not just *the* boss. She is *a* boss. She's navigated male-dominated boardrooms, corporate leadership, and a family by knowing her priorities. She's been quoted as saying, "I'm a mother first, then a CEO." As a leader, she walked the walk (more leaders like Indra, please!). Her daughters' school was ten minutes from the PepsiCo office, and "If there was a problem, I ran over there. It didn't matter if I was in a meeting."[17]

That's not to say she didn't have to work incredibly hard to prove she belonged.

In her memoir *My Life in Full: Work, Family, and Our Future*, Indra describes a few of her experiences working at PepsiCo:

As PepsiCo's chairman for a dozen years, I led our board meetings sitting at the head of a large U-shaped conference table in a sunny corner room. We were eight men and four women. The meetings would begin with friendly greetings and then get down to business. We analyzed performance, risks, strategy, talent, and what we saw across the world. I was lucky to work with a supportive board, but some of the comments in public and private by a board member or two were rude and patronizing, remarks I imagine they wouldn't dare make to a male leader. Additionally, I had to put up with a couple of the men thinking it was OK to talk over me or interrupt me midsentence...

When I was rising in PepsiCo, like many female senior executives, I was also the only woman in the room when our management team sat around debating tactics. I was always well prepared and offered good insight, and I know I was respected. But, quite often when I made suggestions, someone would jump in and say, "Oh no, Indra. That's too theoretical." A few minutes later, a man would suggest the exact same thing, using the same words, and be congratulated for his terrific, insightful idea. I once leaned over to a senior operating executive and loudly asked him to bring up a thought of mine. "Otherwise, it will be viewed as too theoretical," I quipped. That ended the "too theoretical" comments...

I also weighed in with a female perspective on marketing and advertising campaigns. One Diet Pepsi TV commercial in the 1990s sticks in my mind. The setting is a fancy wedding with the bridesmaids and guests waiting around. Something has gone wrong. One woman tells another that the bride's diamond is small, and then it becomes clear that the groom isn't showing up. The resplendent bride is crying. Her father gives her a Diet Pepsi. She sips. She peps up.

She looks at her dad and says, "This is diet?"

I saw this ad in an internal screening and told the creators that I didn't think it would encourage women to drink Diet Pepsi because it was insulting. None of the men agreed. And they were furious that I weighed in, noting that this wasn't my responsibility. The campaign went ahead. Later, a few of those guys actively avoided talking to me about the numbers when Diet Pepsi had a disappointing year.

I made one more memorable, very visible change. I had the beautiful French cobblestones on the walkway between our buildings ripped out in favor of an architecturally tasteful, flat surface. The cobblestones, installed in the late 1960s, were fine for men in business shoes but a menace for women wearing the heels expected of us in our professional wardrobes. The change infuriated Don Kendall, who had retired as CEO in 1986 but kept an office. When he saw the construction, he fumed, "Who's messing up my walkway?" My male colleagues, who had long known those cobblestones were a hazard and seen people struggle and even trip and fall, pointed at me. Why they had never fixed them, I would never know. Don, surprisingly, never dared confront me about it.

My female colleagues, including Don's wife, Bim, thanked me for years for changing those stones.[18]

When asked why there aren't more female CEOs in America, Indra said that "many women don't reach those upper ranks because of the demands of balancing work and family life, in a way many of their male counterparts are not expected to."[19]

In other cases, Indra says women rising through big companies leave to lead smaller companies. For one thing, they can reach that top tier at a smaller company. And, most important, a smaller company will offer more flexibility and a less rigid lifestyle for women who want or have a family. Indra went on to say, "I honestly believe that if we give young family builders and women the appropriate support...we would have more women CEOs."

Later in this book, we'll talk about why becoming a mom equips you with superpowers. Why companies should want women in C-level roles (CEO, CFO, COO). Why companies should be doing everything in their power not only to retain us, but also to attract and celebrate us.

Unfortunately, the American workplace is not set up to support the working mom. In fact, if I were to give the US a grade on how it treats women—especially working moms—today, I'd have to fail us.

Being a working dad works. So why doesn't being a working mom work?

If we're looking at raw data, the pay gap is likely related to the fact that working moms aren't viewed as viable leaders. The US says, "You can create an entire life within your body, but we don't think you're capable of leading a meeting on budget cuts."

> The pay gap is likely related to the fact that working moms aren't viewed as viable leaders.

Working moms aren't as respected as men, or even as respected as women who choose not to have children, so we aren't given the roles that earn the big bucks.

The reasons working moms aren't respected are varied, but it comes down to two main factors: Structural roadblocks exist at a systemic level, and pervasive, outdated mindsets persist about a woman's "place" in the family dynamic, something I've personally struggled with quite a bit. Both of these factors serve to perpetuate inequality in the workplace, and neither appears to have a quick fix.

Another way the US fails working moms is in not making allowances for childcare. Working moms are in a constant struggle to find affordable childcare, and organizations wash their hands of any responsibility to provide support or flexibility to equip working moms to succeed at work and at home. Employers wonder, "Why is this *my* problem?" It's important to cover all sides of this story, and I will.

When female outliers are promoted to high levels of influence, we still experience misogyny and patronizing behavior from our peers. To top it all off, we have to work forty-two extra days to get the same paycheck as men in the same position as ours.

Yes, the situation is bad. If this were a news report, melancholy music would underscore this entire chapter.

Until now. Cue an uptick in tempo. Something inspirational that gets you pumped up and ready for a fight. Your workout playlist. Your I've-got-fourteen-minutes-alone-in-the-car mix. Maybe "Eye of the Tiger" or Lizzo's "Good as Hell." For me, it's Def Leppard's "Pour Some Sugar on Me."

We cannot lose hope. As I've mentioned, the problem is great, but the problem solvers are greater. Awareness is growing. Yours, mine, and the rest of the country's. We can do better. We will do better.

But there's another pit stop we have to make before we start talking about a solution. We need to take a trip together into American history to fully grasp the origin of just how our country got into the shape it's in.

Our destination? The warm and cozy kitchen of June Cleaver herself.

CHAPTER THREE

CARRYING THE LOAD

The hardest part is the mom guilt and the challenge of compartmentalizing things. It's so hard to get into a work flow only to be interrupted about snacks or fights or even harmless updates or asks for attention. It's hard when the kids ask me to play something with them and I'm constantly [saying] "I'm working" or "I have a meeting." It bums me out when they reply "You *always* have a meeting!"

—Gaelyn Jenkins, creative director and mom of two

Before you read this chapter, I want you to know I've struggled with working outside the home. Doesn't a "good" mom stay home with the kids, like my mom did with me and my three siblings? And I didn't just work outside the home; I was the primary breadwinner for many years. These days, well, I'm not sure what I am. I'm home with my kids, but I have side hustles as an independent contractor, founder of CARRY Media, and podcaster. So, I'm staying home, momming, and working.

Working and leading are things I'm passionate about. However, the way I was raised, the messages I heard from faith circles, created an ongoing internal conflict and inner monologue: "Should I even be working? Isn't my place at home?" I tell you this only to admit to you I've been on my own journey.

At points on this journey, I'm ashamed to admit that I once wondered if a woman should be president or if women should be in the military. Wasn't a woman's place in the home? Not in the boardrooms and at the front lines?

Needless to say, I was wrong. I've come a long way. But there's so much more work to be done. I'm committed to it, but we also need some help from the men in our lives to do the work.

MEN AREN'T THE ENEMY

As we peel back the layers of history in our country over this chapter, I want to remind you that I'm not in any way anti-man. In fact, I believe our best advocates are the men in our lives. I'm hopelessly in love with my two young sons. Though much of our patronizing and misogynistic history angers me, I refuse to emasculate men or even blame them. We need our sons, brothers, husbands, and fathers to stand alongside us and champion us. We'll be talking extensively later in the book about how we can invite them into the conversation.

You read earlier about Indra Nooyi's husband being her "life partner" and how he made things possible for their family.

For me, it's been my husband, John, who's made it possible.

He's my biggest advocate and cheerleader. He's supported me and our family, even when it wasn't popular. But the sexiest thing about him, in my opinion, is watching him be actively involved in our kids' lives. (Oh, and when he's making dinner.) What makes John attractive has nothing to do with him bringing home a paycheck—though he's never had a problem doing that either.

I'm starting to realize that the greatest disservice women did to men was telling them generations ago that their sole contribution to a family was to be its financial provider, releasing them from their obligation at home to be involved in their children's lives. Meaning, bring home a paycheck and that's it. As one of the experts I spoke with, Jennifer Glass, told me, "It's *flat-out evil* what [American society] has done to men."

We have all played a part in getting to this point. And we need to work together to find a new way forward. Hand in hand, step by step, we will.

Now, the bandage of truth must come off. And I warn you, it's going to be a bit painful. (Mostly because this bandage implicates *us*—moms.)

> As one of the experts I spoke with, Jennifer Glass, told me, "It's *flat-out evil* what [American society] has done to men."

THE "NUCLEAR" FAMILY

There was a hit TV show in the 1950s called *Father Knows Best*. After starting out as a radio show in the late 1940s, *Father Knows Best* went on to air on TV for six seasons, broadcasting over two hundred black-and-white TV episodes from 1954 to 1960. *Father Knows Best* was essentially a situation comedy that followed the

Anderson family, a white middle-class family in the fictional sub-urban town of Springfield.

In season 2, episode 30, titled "Betty, Girl Engineer," a teenage Betty Anderson attends her high school's career day festivities.[1] As Betty is waiting in line to sign up for an internship in her career field of choice, we see the school counselor dismissively telling the girls before Betty to go ahead and write down "secretary" while patting the back of the young man who signed up for "chemical research."

When it's Betty's turn, she chooses to write down "engineer" instead—much to the chagrin of the counselor and the boy in line behind her, who says, "Betty, look what you wrote down. You can't mean that!" As if a person could accidentally write down an entire word. He exclaims, "But you're a girl!"

Betty's response: "Aren't girls people?"

When Betty announces to her family that she's going to spend her spring vacation interning with the county surveying crew, you'd have thought by her family's reactions that Betty was planning to join a gang. "You're joking," her mother insists, while recommending that Betty try on a pretty dress instead.

Her father calms Betty's panicked mother by saying, "Don't worry, darling. After half a day of trampling through the dirt, she'll be ready to take up some nice vocation…like crocheting."

"I don't even feel like I have a daughter anymore," her mother laments, while her brother refuses to call her by her name, opting for her initials, "BJ," instead.

At Betty's worksite she is introduced to her new boss, Doyle Hobbs. Doyle can't imagine why a girl would be interested in engineering. "Are you trying to get back at a boyfriend?" he demands.

Then come some of the most telling lines from the entire episode. Doyle says, "You're a girl, and a girl has the obligation of being one. The male has his job and the female has hers. Don't confuse them."

And if you just jumped to your feet in a rage, I'm with you. But this really happened. No, this wasn't ironic social commentary. This was the reality of the attitude toward women in the fifties.

Eventually, Betty gives up and returns home, defeated. She puts on that pretty dress her mother has been fussing about and accepts a date with Doyle Hobbs. Betty's father watches happily in the background, grinning like a Cheshire cat.

All is right in his world again.

I wish I could tell you that this episode was satirical and that Betty's family's and Doyle's response to her ambitions to be an engineer were hyperbolic—sarcasm meant to drum up meaningful conversation about a woman's role in society. But that would be a lie. "Betty, Girl Engineer" was a not-so-gentle reminder that even though women had the right to vote, their role was still to be at home, wear pretty dresses, and be the homemakers engineers came home to—homemakers that reminded the men of their mothers.

I believe we're still carrying a lot of these expectations around today.

If you need to go scream into a pillow, I'll wait right here. Throughout the researching and writing of this book, I've found it to be a very effective method. Just promise to come back when your blood pressure stabilizes.

Let's do a quick experiment together. If you were to describe the traditional family unit, what would that list include? Now, before you answer, think about the "ideal" American family. If you were to describe this family to a friend, you'd say, "Oh, you know. They're very traditional."

By the way, this is a no-judgment zone. No one will be scrutinizing how you answer.

I bet a lot of us would say:

Father works. Mother stays home. Both remain faithful in their marriage.

The mother is the caretaker of their two (or three, tops) children, while the father works a steady job to provide. They're not wealthy, but they're not pinching pennies every month, either.

The family lives in a two-story house in a suburban cul-de-sac with affable neighbors they have an annual Super Bowl party with.

There's a dog in there somewhere, and quite possibly a minivan with sports equipment in the trunk.

This is the "American Dream," right? Well, not according to Stephanie Coontz.

Stephanie is a historian and director of research and public education at the Council on Contemporary Families. She has studied the history of American families, marriage, and changes in gender roles longer than most of us have been alive.

In her book *The Way We Never Were: American Families and the Nostalgia Trap*, she discusses the idealized family from the 1950s—the nuclear (in *all* senses of the word) family that many Americans use as a measuring stick for comparison.

I interviewed Coontz for this book, and she tells me this family never existed—not within the vacuum of perfection we imagine. In fact, the picture of the "traditional" family isn't very traditional at all. When people raise their fists and say, "We need to go back to the old ways—to our former family values," they typically mean they want American families to look like the Andersons, the

Cleavers, or similar TV families. But these types of families didn't actually exist in the 1950s (or ever) en masse. Like most television today, the nuclear family was fictional.

And what I've learned throughout the writing of this book is that when we start romanticizing an era, we forget that what seemed good was selective. How? Well, it was only there part of the time for part of the people, and it was often predicated on awful things.

For example, the 1950s we keep dreaming about. Sure, it was easier for a man to support his family on one income. That's because, sadly, Black people and women were excluded from jobs at the time. And if a woman had an ounce of aspiration outside the home or wondered why her husband came home with lipstick on his collar, psychologists would ask her, "Are you keeping yourself well-groomed enough?" They had no options to leave or negotiate. They put up with stuff.

So, let's you and I do something: Let's take a stroll down memory lane. Grab a drink—you'll need it as we examine the American family over the course of history. If you're not a history buff, don't worry. The content is still juicy. In fact, it blew my mind.

NONTRADITIONAL "TRADITIONAL" FAMILIES

The "nuclear" family with a male breadwinner is the most nontraditional family in human history. Unless a family was upper-class and had servants and other hired help, men and women were co-producers and co-laborers in family economies for the vast majority of human existence. Socially, men were in charge and women deferred to their husbands, but in practice, households were managed interdependently. They are still run the same way in many cultures and countries all over the world—just not ours.

The concepts of "men's work" and "women's work" didn't exist. Men more often did long-distance travel and work that required heavy lifting. But records show that although there was division of labor, a woman worked just as hard as a man. She had to till and work the fields as a laborer. She was also in charge of dairying, salting, and butchering the animals. I'll remember that the next time I'm complaining about having to make dinner.

The Original Hipsters

A sixteenth-century brewery[2]

In the medieval period, women were master brewers. Beer brewers. That's right, the women were in charge of the fermentation process to provide beer for religious ceremonies and for meals at home. Beer was economical, and it was a way to consume and preserve grains—not to mention it was a decent source of carbs and proteins to recharge after those long days on the farm (explaining why so much of it was consumed!). Many women took their brewing skills to the marketplace. In other words, medieval women were the original hipsters.

I recently walked into a bar. And before you ask, no, this isn't a cheesy joke involving a priest and two unlikely drinking buddies. I literally entered an establishment with a bar. Behind the counter was a sign that said, "Throughout nearly all of beer's history, it was brewed almost exclusively by a woman." I'll toast to that.

In addition to brewers, medieval women were also spinners, dairyers, candlemakers, and fan makers. No, women weren't "equal" in the work world, but women were respected because they were productive members of the household and community. When women described themselves in this time period, they used words like *industrious* and *hardworking*, not yet needing to identify as the primary "nurturers" of the household.

Per Coontz, there's plenty of evidence to suggest that men saw their wives as perfectly competent to negotiate anything if they were gone. To take it one step further, women would often take over their husband's trade—butchers and blacksmiths—if their husband died. They were prepared to do so because they were working alongside them much of the time.

But in terms of work, there was no separation of "home life" and "work life." They were the same. Work life *was* home life and vice versa. There was no "breadwinner." No parent was a stay-at-home parent. Everyone worked to contribute to the household, especially when it came to raising the children.

Let's take a look at how the American family dynamic has changed over the years, starting with America's first families.

America's First Families

"THE GOLDEN PUMPKIN, NUGGET OF THE FIELD."

Families in the colonies. Credit: iStockphoto / PennyLens[3]

The female experience in the colonial era (circa 1600–1775) varied from colony to colony and was largely influenced by socio-economic status and ethnicity.

Though the narrative of this time period often centers around witch hunts and a revolution led by men, middle-class colonial women played a significant role in society. Most colonial women were married, and the term *goodwife* was commonly used. A code of ethics governed female life in the colonies from 1650 to 1750. Goodwives had legal rights in colonial America, and actually had more freedom than women in the 1800s would have.[4]

Women continued in trades of their own, worked on the farms, or helped their husbands with their trades. Wives were expected to be subservient to their husbands, and men were no doubt the dominant gender. Along with their household duties or trades, women were expected to raise good, God-fearing kids who mastered a trade or skill that was socially appropriate for their class and gender.

Enter the great disturbance—the Industrial Revolution.

American Families in the Industrial Revolution and Victorian Era

Victorian family. Credit: iStockphoto / ArtMarie[5]

As demand for food and goods grew after a population surge in the early 1800s, so did the use of more efficient machinery to increase supply and cut down on labor costs. The Industrial Revolution reached its height in the US around 1830, replacing the need for much of the existing manual labor. Paid work moved outside of the home and into the cities.

Stephanie Coontz writes, "A new division of labor by age and sex emerged among the middle class." Instead of working side by side with their husbands on the family farm or managing a skill or trade, "[w]omen's roles were refined in terms of domesticity rather than production, men were labeled as 'breadwinners' (a masculine identity unheard of in the colonial days), children were said to need time to play, and gentle maternal guidance supplanted the patriarchal authoritarianism of the past."[6]

Sound dreamy? Not so much.

Slave, child, and immigrant labor saw significant increases during this time, and working conditions were horrific. Think twelve-hour days in the coal mines or body parts getting mutilated, with no recourse, by factory equipment. Coontz says, "In 1900, 120,000 children worked in Pennsylvania mines and factories; most of them had started work by age eleven," while "[c]hildren made up 23.7 percent of the 36,415 workers in southern textile mills around the turn of the century."[7]

Girls were raised to prepare for marriage, with an emphasis on learning "feminine" skills like washing, sewing, cooking, and weaving. Once married, women were expected to stay out of "worldly" issues and focus on creating comfortable homes for their husbands. A lack of viable contraceptive methods meant married women had very little control over their bodies throughout the childbearing years (did I mention a population boom?).

Women did not spend much time with their children, leaving those duties to nannies or older daughters.

Let me repeat that again.

Women did not spend much time with their children. And they did not feel guilty about it—not one bit.

But with their husbands commuting to work in the city and not being as present in the home, women had to take on more unpaid work than ever, carrying the load of the household duties and the children with or without help.

To be clear, there were expectations for men as well. Men were to be "involved [in] detaching oneself from the home and its feminine comforts" and concentrated on "a level of material success in the wider world" including "the recognition of manhood by one's peers."[8]

Men were expected to gain the admiration not only of women, but of their peers as well. They were to be married to a suitable woman, father as many children as possible, be high earners outside the home, and exert their masculinity by lording over all beneath their respective roofs.

By the end of the nineteenth century, the members of America's high society decided that family values had been destroyed by the Industrial Revolution: "Reformers advocated for adoption of a 'true American' family—a restricted, exclusive nuclear unit in which women and children were divorced from the world of work."[9]

The Great Depression

My Gido and Sito, Lebanese immigrants, circa 1930, in Flint, Michigan. Pictured: George and Mary Faris. Children: Joseph, Helen, Raymond, and Phil. My dad, Ed Faris, and Aunt Josie hadn't yet been born.

The Great Depression (1929–1939) ushered in yet another new family dynamic. With most American families struggling to survive, many combined their households with relatives as a means of survival, seemingly revitalizing the multigenerational family ties of the past.

But when you peeled back the curtain of returning to older, "better" values, families were doing what they could to simply eat and live. Coontz explains, "Men withdrew from family life or turned violent; women exhausted themselves trying to 'take up the slack' both financially and emotionally, or they belittled their husbands as failures; and children gave up their dreams of education to work at dead-end jobs."[10]

Though both of my parents were born at the tail end of the Great Depression, there's not much to miss about the Great Depression family.

The 1950s American Family

Family dinner. Credit: iStockphoto / Stockbyte[11]

Which brings us to the post–World War II American family. This is the family of Betty, the engineer—the family we most often pine after politically and socially. And, on the surface, why wouldn't we?

> The 1950s was a pro-family period if there ever was one. Rates of divorce and illegitimacy were tiny compared to today; marriage was almost universally praised; the family was everywhere hailed as the most basic institution in society; and a massive baby boom, among all classes and ethnic groups, made America a "child-centered" society.[12]

Judging by the television shows of the time, the typical American family centered around the idea that home was a refuge of safety, even when the outside world was not. There was a bread-winning, rule-enforcing father who kept everyone (even his wife) out of mischief, and a devoted housewife who was completely fulfilled to revolve around the isolated orbits of her kids and husband. Speaking of the kids, they were intelligent and attractive and never got into very much trouble—or at least any trouble that a stern lecture from Dad couldn't straighten out.

Sounds pretty good, right? Keep reading.

The American family of the 1950s was a novel ideal. Men had just returned from war, and it was as if American families sought to redefine what it looked like to live together after the Depression. American families overall had more buying power than ever before. The economy rebounded after the war, and economic prosperity grew. Couples started getting married earlier, having children earlier, and spending more time together as husband and wife after the children left the home.

Films, shows, and plays like *Marty*, *Father Knows Best*, and *Leave it to Beaver* depicted families working together to solve problems, which almost always resulted in a "win" for the nuclear family. But not all was as kosher in suburbia as June Cleaver led us to believe. The cult of domesticity that began in the Victorian era made a comeback.

THE BIRTH OF AMERICAN MOM GUILT

There's a magazine photo of a famous actress at the time, Joan Crawford, doing her own housework, cleaning the floors. Housework was how women found their identity—they could work, but housework was the most important. And they had to do it for themselves; otherwise, they felt like a failure or were seen as weak.

An extensive article in *Screen Guide* in 1950 teases their readers by writing: "Her name is familiar to everyone—but you might not know about the Joan we bring you in this story." The Joan they are bringing is a Joan Crawford who is just like any other person. She opens the door in a cotton housedress, does her own laundry, and goes down on her hands and knees to scrub the kitchen floor. It even tells a nice story of how one time she couldn't sleep because she didn't hang her gown properly.[13]

The 1950s woman based her worth on how brightly the grout between her kitchen tiles shined: "1800s middle-class women had cheerfully left housework to servants, yet 1950s women of all classes created make-work in their homes and felt guilt when they did not do everything for themselves." Cringing yet? Just wait until you hear this: "The amount of time women spent doing housework actually *increased* during the 1950s, despite the advent of convenience foods and new, labor-saving appliances; child care absorbed more than twice as much time as it had in the 1920s."[14]

Why? Well. Maybe it wasn't *all* the housewife's fault. When thousands of American men left to fight the war, women stepped into the public workforce, really for the first time in our country's history. These women learned new skills, joined unions, and formed professional identities. Although 95 percent of the new female employees expected to quit by the end of the war, by the end of 1945, an "overwhelming majority" did not want to give up on their newfound independence and freedom (not to mention their own income) and expressed a desire to keep working.[15]

But once the men returned home, they needed their jobs back. So these excited, fulfilled, and empowered women were once again asked to mold their lives around the needs and wants of men, either by their husbands' demands that they resign and resume their roles as full-time homemakers, or by being downgraded to "female" jobs—or just plain fired. Still, nearly 2 million more wives were employed outside the home in 1952 than in prewar times. "The jobs available to these women, however, lacked the pay and the challenge that had made wartime work so satisfying, encouraging women to define themselves in terms of home and family even when they were working."[16]

Sound familiar?

Women were left with little choice but to retreat back to their ovens and aprons to reprise their Victorian role as homemakers. But these homemakers had some requirements to "qualify" for the newly coveted title.

For the most part, the 1950s homemaker was a middle-class woman with little education. Her parents had sent her to school to get a good husband, while they sent her brother to school to find a good job. The 1950s homemaker may have worked a few years to put her husband through some sort of training, certification, or higher education. *These* women got an extra gold star—tremendous sacrifice was the banner of the 1950s housewife.

She didn't question her husband—not even if he came home with lipstick on his collar. She doted on her children. She occasionally met another housewife to share recipes and local gossip. But most of all, she housewifed. She took care of the home, and she took care of her husband.

Google knows a lot. I searched "1950s housewife duties" and up popped a jaw-dropping list of household chores that *Good Housekeeping*[17] suggested a 1950s housewife adapt for her home and family. The following list also showed up, compiled from contemporaneous housekeeping books:[18]

WEEKLY CHORES

1. Throw back the covers and let your bed air out.
2. Open up the blinds and windows.
3. After breakfast, clean up the kitchen and eating area.
4. Gather a basket for tidying. As you tidy the home, pick up items that don't belong in that room and add them to your basket. When you enter a new room, place the items from the basket that belong in that room where they go.
5. Straighten up the living areas, pick up clutter, lightly dust, straighten pillows, and water plants.
6. Make the beds.
7. Tidy the bedroom, including a light dusting.
8. Hang up any clothes that may be about or ensure dirty ones are in the hamper.
9. Do a light tidy of the bathroom including removing

and replacing used towels, refilling toilet paper and soap (as needed), and cleaning the sink area including soap dishes.

10. Wipe down kitchen work surfaces and inside the fridge and discard any old food.
11. Dispose of garbage from around the home.
12. Rinse dishcloths and hang them to dry.
13. Sweep or mop the kitchen floor.
14. Handle weekly chores that need to be done that day (see examples below).
15. Set the table for dinner.
16. Arrange the living room for evening enjoyment with the family.
17. Do a quick sweep of the floors and ensure entrance ways are clear.
18. Clean up the eating areas after dinner and ensure all dishes are washed.
19. Set the table for breakfast.

ONCE-A-WEEK CHORES

1. Use metal polish on bathroom fixtures.
2. Clean and disinfect all kitchen appliances.
3. Scald and disinfect bread boxes and garbage pails and bins.
4. Replace flowers with fresh bouquets.
5. Laundry (including bedding).
6. Vacuuming and mopping.

I'm exhausted just reading that list. It took about fifty-seven hours a week on average.

I see zero Starbucks runs or trips to McDonald's on those lists. I also don't see when she runs carpool, drops off the forgotten science project at school, answers emails, runs the Zoom meeting, spends time with her children, or, frankly, when she breathes.

You can picture her, can't you? The curl of her hair, the red of her lips. But that smile she's wearing looks a bit forced, doesn't it?

The truth is that our televisions have lied to us.

Nostalgia pulls a fast one on us, *every time*.

The nuclear family of the 1950s was not, in fact, nearly as wholesome and happy-go-lucky as its fictional characters would suggest. For starters, a quarter of Americans were still quite poor: 40 to 50 million people lived below the poverty line. Without the assistance of government aid programs, that number rose by the early 1960s to one-third of the country, especially in the demographics of children and elderly. Even if we focus on "only native-born, white families, one-third could not get by on the income of the household head."[19]

Remember my earlier comment about how what seemed good was selective because it was only there part of the time for part of the people, and often based on horrible things? Yep.

The 1950s saw a massive influx of immigrants from all over the world, especially Mexico. Most nonwhite citizens lived in rural areas prior to the war. With the rise of the civil rights movement of the 1960s, many Black people had moved from the South to the North, 80 percent of Mexicans and Black people lived in cities, and there were more Puerto Ricans in New York city than in San Juan.[20]

As you might imagine, these minority groups did not enjoy the same privileges and wealth as their middle-class white peers. There were no Black or Native American or Mexican families playing in slapstick sitcoms. Over half of Black families lived below the poverty line, while migrant workers suffered "almost medieval" working conditions. The government enforced relocation and termination policies to force Native Americans to give up their treaty rights.[21] In addition:

> African Americans in the South faced systemic, legally sanctioned segregation and pervasive brutality, and those in the North were excluded by restrictive covenants and redlining from many benefits of the economic expansion that their labor helped sustain. Whites resisted, with harassment and violence, the attempts of blacks to participate in the American family dream.[22]

Teen pregnancy rates soared in the 1950s. This legitimately shocked me. While everyone was busy pretending not to notice the dysfunction of their ivory ideals and denying the increasing number of nonwhites being systemically marginalized, they also endeavored to imagine that their teenagers did *not* have healthy, growing, hormonal bodies. A lack of dialogue existed regarding sex at all, much less safe sex. The baby boom of the fifties was a *teenage* baby boom, with a national all-time high of 96 births for every 1,000 among unwed girls aged fifteen to nineteen.[23]

Women of the 1950s were generally mistrusted; in fact, ambitious women were thought to be crazy. Sadly, "psychiatrists in that era insisted that the 'normal' woman found complete fulfillment by renouncing her personal aspirations and identifying with her husband's achievements."[24] It stands to reason that when women entered the labor force—you know, to keep the country running—and found enjoyment and even fulfillment from that work, she became a source of worry and concern for men.

THE DANGER OF NOSTALGIA

Romanticizing the past, particularly the 1950s, is dangerous.

Nostalgia is based on selective memory. We want the feeling, but don't want to go back there.

When you start romanticizing an era, you forget that what seemed good was selective. It was only good part of the time, for part of the people, and often predicated on things that were terrible. In the fifties, it was easier for a man to support a family on one income. Mostly because Black people and women were excluded from jobs at the time.

But we were more moral back then, right? That's what I've always presumed. My presumptions were wrong. Our culture was more disapproving of premarital sex, and society was far less sexualized. However, there was a whole lot of infidelity going on that women were expected to put up with. Ever watched the show *Mad Men*? Case in point. That lipstick the wives found on their husbands' collars? Well, what choice did they have but to scrub it off? It's not like they could get a job and survive on their own income.

And the way we treated minorities and marginalized members of our society?

Trauma therapist and life coach Anita Phillips sits on the advisory board for CARRY Media as a mental health expert. As a white woman, I am fully aware that my perspective is limited. I asked Phillips, a Black woman, to evaluate our content through the lens of her own personal experiences.

"The term 'working mother' itself has institutionalized racism at its core," she said. "'Working' mother suggests a deviation from the norm; a norm established by white men for white women. Black women in America have always worked—first by force and then by overwhelming necessity. Growing up, I never heard the phrase 'working mom' used as a distinguisher in the Black community. My father and my mother worked. I didn't know a black mother who didn't work. Both of our parents worked."

> "The term 'working mother' itself has institutionalized racism at its core."

Phillips's response was not only an education on the institutionalization of language in America but also a reminder of how dangerous "nostalgia" can be. We're told we need a return to the "good old" days, but they were only good to the few because they were built on the backs of the marginalized.

There were other systemic moral failures in the 1950s. The way we responded to domestic violence, the way we covered up incest, and, by the way, rape was *legal* within marriage? It was the "golden age" for precious few.

> A 1954 article in *Esquire* called working wives a "menace."

A 1954 article in *Esquire* called working wives a "menace." A *Life* author termed married women's employment a "disease."[25]

Similar to laws made to restrict the rights and mobility of minorities, women were actively legislated against, with some states going as far as giving the husband complete control over the family's finances.[26]

And it wasn't just women who were held to the idyllic standards of a nuclear family. As difficult as it may be for some to admit or believe, men experienced societal pressures too. As you can imagine, coming out of the Great Depression, there was an emphasis on financial security and stability. A man's one job in life was to earn and provide. If he wasn't able to do so on his own, and his wife had to work outside the home to supplement his income, he was not considered a "real" man.

Gender roles were more defined than ever before, especially in TV and film. The fathers of the family practically woke up in a business suit. They ate a reasonable breakfast prepared by their doting wives, kissed her and the kids on the foreheads, and left for the day to join their peers in the American rat race. Then, when they returned home, they were expected to solve all the problems that had cropped up in their absence with levity and charm.

Could it be that the same societal standards that have asked women to carry it all have also asked men to carry it all too? On top of that, have society's expectations turned into a toxic cycle, one feeding into another? A man wasn't a "real man" unless he held dominion over his wife and kids. The rigidity of the masculinity taught to the boys of the 1950s communicated that devaluing women was perhaps the only way to protect one's own name and manhood.

The American family wasn't defined in this era. The American family was distorted.

AN AHA MOMENT

Let's take a moment to review.

In colonial American families, women had few rights. Minorities had no rights prior to the abolishment of slavery in 1865. It was a strictly patriarchal society, with men and women working side by side to provide and care for their families.

The Victorian family that resulted from the Industrial Revolution, if anything, served to reinforce the dominance of men over their home while causing separation in the family unit by moving most of the work off the farms and fields and into cities. Women were tasked with carrying the weight of teaching and caring for the children, while also maintaining their homes. Women who did enter the workforce did so out of dire necessity and were not paid the same wages as men in the same roles.[27]

The families of the Great Depression were units of interdependence and survival. Multigenerational households increased as parents and grandparents relied on one another to make ends meet. Women entered the workforce in larger numbers to supplement meager incomes. Many women were also tasked with carrying the household duties, which now included patching clothes, stretching meals, and keeping kitchen gardens on top of caring for the children and older parents present in the home. Women were paid much lower rates than men.

I asked my mom, born in 1939, about growing up in St. Louis during the Great Depression. "My mom didn't graduate from high school," she said, "but she did attend a sort of 'business school' when she was fifteen that taught girls how to type and take notes in shorthand."

For some of my mom's life, her mother (my grandmother) was able to stay home with her six children. When times got tough, my grandmother went back to work. "That's when my dad's two sisters and my dad's father helped out watching us kids," Mom said. "My mom would go to work one shift earlier in the morning, and then Dad would come home and take over and finish cooking the dinner while Mom had gotten it started. So the kids were never alone."

The Great Depression was a unique era for our country. Families returned to some of the earlier, communal ways of living, with kids pitching in by either quitting school and going to work or by contributing to the household duties. "We would scrub the kitchen floor," my mom said of her chores growing up. "Sweep. Take the bucket down to the outhouse. I used to go to the grocery store for my mom. We had a corner market. You could get everything there. You could get your meat, vegetables, and canned goods—stuff like that. And I would go to the grocery store for my mom with a little wicker basket and bring everything back."

My mom recalled a time when the groceries accidentally became a feline's feast. "One time when I came home from the store, instead of taking the groceries back upstairs to our apartment on the third floor, I sat them down on the bottom step because the kids were playing something and I wanted to join in. I came back and found the kitty cat had gotten into the food. Nothing was salvageable."

I don't know why I love this story so much. Maybe it's because even though culture and circumstances are constantly in flux, kids are always kids.

The postwar American family emerged as a picturesque, sparkling embodiment of the newly defined American Dream. Select white men prospered in the workplace, while women experienced an identity crisis as they were forced or guilted into returning home after carrying the weight of the labor and home while their husbands were away at war. Minorities had few rights and experienced discrimination and abuse in their everyday lives. The teenage baby boom forced marriage or ostracization on young mothers. And reports of domestic abuse and rape went largely unreported or not investigated.[28]

Meantime, in post–World War II Europe, women were treated much differently, mainly out of necessity. They lost so many men—much of their workforce—in the war. With two huge issues to solve, they turned to moms. Moms needed to replace the lost souls by procreating. But they also were needed in the workplace because of labor shortages. So they had to create a work structure that supported them as moms and laborers. That's why many European countries have such superior family leave polices and offer early childhood education and affordable childcare. If they hadn't, they would have lost their laborers.

What a stark contrast to how we handled things here in the US. So, how *did* we get here?

At different time periods, across different classes and regions, as men moved out of the home to the permanent workforce, it made more sense for women to take on more of the household duties. Men earned more. It was simple math.

Previously, women had been in charge of the children only during infancy, when they were nursing, and the men were in charge of their children's moral instruction until they left the home. But as men continued to spend more hours working outside the home, women, by default, began meeting the majority of their kids' emotional needs. Women began to internalize the idea that nurturing was not only what they were good at, but maybe even *all* they were good at. Men, in turn, began refusing to do childcare or housework, internalizing the idea that the only things they were good at were providing and protecting.

Uncovering this was an aha moment for me in the writing of this book.

As time went on, it became increasingly difficult for families to survive on one income. In addition, women became restless behind the gates of the front doors. So, women decided to master both realms—home life *and* work life. We decided our only choice at fulfillment was to carry it all.

You know what they say about hindsight being 20/20? For some reason, that principle has failed us as a country when we consider the American family. Or maybe *we've* failed *it*. For the last two centuries, we've struggled with an ostentatious gender gap. A racial gap, too, but for the purposes of this book, we'll focus on the relationship between men and women, concentrating on the working mom.

As a society, we've asked women to carry the slack. Then we've sent them mixed messages about their performance, identity, and worth. We've asked women to work outside the home, paid them less, provided them with little to no support or tools to handle the weight of all they're carrying, then we've shamed them for having the nerve to enjoy it.

Hey, ladies: Work like you don't have children, and raise children as if you don't work.

As the "golden age" melted into the fight for the rights of women and minorities, parental time with children was on the decline between 1965 and 1975 as women entered the workforce again as the cost of living rose. "In that era, fathers had not yet stepped up to the plate at home, and families were struggling to find a new equilibrium."[29]

Statistically, today's single and working moms spend more time with their children than married homemaker mothers did back in 1965.

I think this bears repeating: You are spending more time with your kids than married homemakers did in 1965.

No, you're not a 1950s housewife. But Mama, you are doing well. Data says so! In 2016, moms spent around twenty-five hours a week on paid work, up from nine hours in 1965. At the same time, they spent fourteen hours a week on childcare, up from ten hours a week in 1965.[30]

Mom shaming isn't my jam—it's not that the moms of the fifties and sixties did a bad job. I'm sure those moms were doing the best they could with what resources, support, and tools they were given. Because that's what we do as moms. We figure it out. The house, the calendar, the dinner, the kids—all of it. And maybe, just maybe, we're doing better than we think we are. Not *maybe*, in fact. We are!

Let's make an agreement right now, you and I. First of all, let's stop comparing ourselves to "traditional" families, wives, and mothers. We no longer romanticize a TV family that never really existed. Let's agree that the data shows that although there are gender gaps, they have gotten slightly smaller over the years. Let's agree that *we* have the power to push those gaps closed for the children we're raising.

Let's agree not to carry the façade of the past into the present one day more.

> Let's stop comparing ourselves to "traditional" families, wives, and mothers. We no longer romanticize a TV family that never really existed.

CHAPTER FOUR

THE SHOW MUST CARRY ON

Recently, I had someone tell me that I do too much and I am not taking care of my kids. This person sees only my work online and does not see what I do throughout the day. They assume because I am working, I am neglecting my kids. I have received comments such as "You can't save them all!," and "You need to be there for your kids because they will be gone," and "You are doing too much; you are going to collapse." What frustrates me is this: when do we hear anyone say to a man "You are working too much at work. We watch you work all day and then come home and take care of your family. Man, you really need to slow down and take care of yourself"?

—Jenn, nonprofit ministry founder and mom of four

I was getting ready to receive the Philip Habib Award for Distinguished Public Service in DC from the American Task Force on Lebanon (I'm half Lebanese). This award was a big deal to me. My grandparents immigrated to the United States with the clothes on their backs and not much else. They set the standard for me for what it means to work hard and make sacrifices for your family. I wouldn't be here without my Gido and Sito (Arabic for *Grandfather* and *Grandmother*). I owe them everything.

I had flown my parents in from Michigan and spent an extravagant amount of money on a designer dress whose brand I can't even pronounce. I even had my colleague and all-around badass Martha Raddatz flown in to introduce me. I woke up the day of the event and immediately knew something was off with my body.

Then, about thirty minutes before I was scheduled to speak and receive the award, I ran in the bathroom, held my perfectly coiffed hair away from my best-I-could-do makeup job, and I vomited until my stomach hurt. When there was absolutely nothing left, I went to the mirror, brushed my teeth with my finger, and returned to the banquet.

A short time later, I spoke onstage to thousands of people. If they had only seen me hunched over the toilet just before…Let's be thankful for all parties involved they had not.

I didn't know a video of my acceptance speech existed until we decided to write about it for this book. I was cringing when I first watched it, but it wasn't as bad as it felt in the moment. The average person wouldn't have known I'd just been puking my guts out. But that's what moms do quite well. We put on a happy face, smile, and tell ourselves we're fine, when in reality, we're not.

When I think back on this story, it doesn't seem that

outstanding to me or even very special. But when I share it, some people are like, "Paula! What? How? Why?" And I shrug.

This is what we *do* as moms in America. We get the job done, whatever the cost. We meet the expectations, whatever the cost. We wipe the vomit off our chins and go accept international awards, whatever the cost. The show must go on, right?

But what if the cost of carrying the show is our happiness? What if the cost of carrying the show is our self-respect? What if the cost of carrying the show is to reach the end of our lives and think, *Wait…that's it?*

DISHWASHERS FROM OUTER SPACE

Before I go pointing fingers, let me start with myself. *I'm part of the problem.* I need to start teaching my boys to contribute. I love what Ruth Chou Simons does with her boys. Ruth is the CEO of GraceLaced, an art and lifestyle brand, as well as an author, speaker, and mama to six boys. She also happens to be a dear friend. On one of her Instagram posts, Ruth shared this:

Buy a deep freezer and teach [your sons] how to cook.

IN CASE YOU'RE WONDERING:

Boys can be rowdy AND respectful, masculine and tender hearted, into dirt bikes and into crafts. They can hold their mama's hand long after it's cool to do so, and they CAN learn to converse about their feelings. Boys can cook, clean, and follow their mamas around Anthropologie. Boys can admire their dads AND their moms, and find something to emulate in each. They can seek adventure and still want you to ask them out on a dinner date.

Ruth's boys clean, and they do their own laundry and the majority of the cooking. I was so intrigued about how she manages to get her boys to buy in.

She tells me that the most important thing is to be on mission as a family. Let them know they have a part in it and teach them the joy of responsibility.

And then, moms and dads, we have to let our kids fail. "Sometimes we don't have our kids do the work in the home because we think we can do it faster and better. It's too much work. It's inefficient to have a young person try to cut vegetables or do their own laundry—it might not turn out great."

I'm guilty of that, for sure.

There's a learning curve, and Ruth shared a hilarious story about that curve. One of her boys was learning how to do his laundry and forgot to rinse the "racing stripe" out of his underwear. When he started folding the laundry, he discovered a brown ball that looked like a chocolate truffle. "It had collected every scrap of lint in the wash, rolling and tossing, until there was a perfectly shaped, one-inch chocolate truffle." It took a while, but they soon figured out what that truffle was.

Ruth, I admire you. I want to be like you. But I'll never ever in the history of time be able to eat another chocolate truffle.

Meantime, in my casa, I've said on more than one occasion to my two boys that I'll do their laundry until they're fifty and they can live with us as long as they want. As for my daughter? I know she's strong and capable like me—so she can figure it all out. Thus, I've never offered those options to her. Not once. I would have nursed my boys as long as they'd wanted. But sadly, they were both done around a year. (I know, I have issues.)

I'm slowly getting better. I have to—we have to. Recent stud-ies[1] show that although young men are more accepting today of women working outside the home, and even accepting of women holding high-ranking positions within organizations, they are still less likely to equally divide the household chores and childcare. They're happy for us to carry it all.

As much as we want to nur-ture our kids, there's a point where we're cutting them off at the knees. I see this happen a lot in mothers of boys. There's a unique connec-tion between a mother and son— one that makes us want to nurture them and keep them close as long and as much as possible.

But ultimately, that's an almost selfish impulse and doesn't give us the results that we really want. It may fill our cup as mothers, but it pokes a hole in theirs. Like it or not, sons leave our homes just like our daughters do. Boys want to become men. And when we allow them to be boys longer than we should, we're doing them a disservice.

> Recent studies show that although young men are more accepting today of women working outside the home, and even accepting of women holding high-ranking positions within organizations, they are still less likely to equally divide the household chores and childcare. They're happy for us to carry it all.

When my sons find their partners, I want them to be *partners*. I don't want them to look at a dishwasher like it just landed in their kitchen from outer space. I want my kids' future partners to thank me for empowering independent, thoughtful, and kind humans.

MOM GUILT

One of the best parts of my work with CARRY Media is that I get to meet working moms from all over the world and hear their stories. One question I like to ask is, "What resonates most with you? Mom guilt? Burnout? Exhaustion? Or just the feeling that you're never quite nailing it?"

In one of these interviews, I met Chicago working mom Laura Maychruk. Laura is a restaurant owner, Realtor, and mom to four. Here's how Laura answered that question: "I would say for me, I am always feeling not quite enough in all of my worlds. I am trying to be the absolute best at work, in the restaurant, as a Realtor, as a mom. And I'm feeling like I could always do better in every single situation."

I asked, "How do you feel like you could do better? What would that feel like for you?"

Laura didn't have to think. It was as if she'd been thinking these thoughts on repeat: "I wish I could be there more for the people I care about. I feel like probably my biggest mom guilt is my ability or my inability to do thoughtful things for others. When people—my friends, my kids, my husband—want to tell me about things, I wish I could be more in that moment."

Laura went on to describe how she never felt like she was hitting a home run, and often felt as if she were hanging on by a thread. And *ugh*—moms, we can all relate, right?

I asked her, "If you were to describe to someone what it's really like to be a working mom in America, what would you say?"

What Laura said next sent me on another investigative journey—one that peeled back one more layer of the working mom onion. She said, "That's an interesting question, because I have exchange students from around the world that have come and lived with me and seen American motherhood. And more than one exchange student from more than one country has said, 'American mothers work harder than any mother in the world.' Because we take on more than any mother does. We don't have help. We don't have family living in our houses. We take on the responsibilities of the home, the children, and we are working outside of the home. That's an American problem. It's not a worldwide problem."

When I finished my interview with Laura, I absolutely knew I had discovered another piece to the puzzle of why being a working mom in America doesn't work. Why we're burned out as heck and, in Laura's words, "hanging on by a thread."

I asked my friend and former *View* co-host Sherri Shepherd to rank her mom guilt on a scale of zero to ten. Sherri said, "It's a 9.5. [My son] Jeffrey asked me one night in frustration, 'Why can't you be like other moms and stay home?' It broke my heart, because I am a single mom taking care of all the bills and his special needs, school fees, therapy, etc.; a dad with Alzheimer's. If I don't work and bring in a paycheck, the entire house of cards will fall. And being a single mom in the entertainment industry, I always have to hustle to keep working. Stand-up comedy, speaking, hosting talk shows—all require me to travel—and Jeffrey is in school, so he can't travel with me. I just hope one day he will look up and realize that I made a lot of sacrifices for him and that I did what I loved."

Mom guilt is no respecter of status, race, paycheck, or marital status. If you're a working mom in America, it will find you. Why? Why can't we find more joy and less shame in our ultimate purpose on this planet: motherhood?

> Mom guilt is no respecter of status, race, paycheck, or marital status. If you're a working mom in America, it will find you.

For one, I think that we're doing it wrong. We are. I am. You are. Working moms in America. We're trying to carry it all, but that's not how it has to be. At least, that's not how working mothers in other countries parent. And guess what. They're happier. Their families enjoy more quality time together. And they rank higher in terms of mental and physical health.

What? Why? How? I know. That's how I felt too.

Being a working mom isn't easy in any country. But the data and the people tell us that in America, it's simply more challenging.

"HOT-HOUSED" CHILDREN

We've already established that we're still wrestling with a romanticization of the 1950s nuclear family. Yes, even today. Women are being asked to carry it all—and with a smile on their face.

In a time where women make up nearly half the country's labor force and men are more involved in housework and childcare than in the recent past (shout-out to you awesome dads!), the public sees vastly different pressure points for women and men in today's American society.

"Roughly eight-in-ten adults (77%) say women face a lot of pressure to be an involved parent; a significantly smaller share (49%) says the same about men. In contrast, most adults (76%) say men face a lot of pressure to support their family financially, while only 40% say women face this type of pressure."[2]

Here's what we've found in our CARRY Media research: Approximately 70 percent of working mothers in America are working for the paycheck.

> Approximately 70% of working mothers in America are working for the paycheck.

I love our country. I believe America to be the greatest nation on the entire planet. But we're young. We're teenagers in country years! And like a lot of teenagers, we tend to think we know best. My teen daughter will most definitely resent that I just wrote that. (Caroline, I love and respect you! XO!)

We don't have the wisdom or experience of European nations. And instead of looking at how these places do work/life balance, we use our own national reflection to gauge our values, habits, and beliefs.

Let's get outside of our borders. Let's look at what other countries are doing (and not doing). These are the countries who have smaller "happy gaps" between parents and non-parents. These are the countries where "mom guilt" is *not* part of the vernacular. These are the countries where being a working mom works.

Let's start with the obvious. Why are more moms entering the workforce than ever before in our country? Yes, inflation is a real thing, especially in a post-COVID-19 marketplace. But also, Americans love to spend—on ourselves, but especially on our kids. And not just our money. We like to spend our time. In an article[3] on the subject, the *New Yorker* made the following observations: "With the exception of the imperial offspring of the Ming dynasty and the dauphins of pre-Revolutionary France, contemporary American kids may represent the most indulged young people in the history of the world."

The article went on to support their assertion, ticking off "stuff" we give our kids: "clothes, toys, cameras, skis, computers, televisions, cell phones, PlayStations, iPods. (The market for Burberry Baby and other forms of kiddie 'couture' has reportedly been growing by ten percent a year.)"

According to professors of psychology Jean Twenge and

W. Keith Campbell, American children have also been given unprecedented authority: "Parents want their kids' approval, a reversal of the past ideal of children striving for their parents' approval."[4]

The *New Yorker* article goes on: "In many middle-class families, children have one, two, sometimes three adults at their beck and call. This is a social experiment on a grand scale, and a growing number of adults fear that it isn't working out so well: According to one poll, commissioned by *Time* and CNN, two-thirds of American parents think that their children are spoiled."[5]

OK. Ouch. But also, *sort of true*. Just like I am tempted to do with my boys, have we as parents burned up some energy overparenting?

I came across an article put out by the BBC titled "American Parenting Styles Sweep Europe."[6] It opened my eyes to the global perspective of what it's like to raise kids in America: "The US preference [in parenting style] represents the shift that has taken place in the way American parents raise their children; the transition from the so-called latchkey kids of the 1980s to the helicoptered and hot-housed children of today."

"Hot-housed" children? That's a new one. They're defined as children who are rigorously pushed to excel academically faster than what is cognitively and intellectually appropriate for the child's age.[7] Newsflash: This is *not* a compliment on our parenting. We are pushing our kids just as hard as we're pushing ourselves.

> We are pushing our kids just as hard as we're pushing ourselves.

The article goes on to say that "parenting in European nations has traditionally been more relaxed, yet...more parents are adopting the kind of intensive parenting style common in the US."

In an article for National Public Radio,

columnist Emily Lodish discusses global parenting habits that have *not* caught on in the US.[8]

Take my hand, okay? We're about to step out of our American bubbles together.

1. Kids nap outside in Norway, even in freezing temperatures. Toddlers spend a ton of time outside at Barnehage, even in extremely cold temperatures. It's not uncommon to see kids bundled up outside during a Scandinavian winter, taking a nap in their strollers.

2. Parents in Vietnam typically potty-train their children by nine months using a kind of Pavlovian approach. They teach their babies to pee on command by using a whistling noise.

3. The Kisii people of Kenya avoid direct eye contact with their babies. That probably sounds a little extreme, but in the Kisii culture, eye contact conveys that the other person has power, which is not what Kisii parents want to project to their children.

4. In Denmark, children are often left outside to get fresh air while their caregiver goes into a restaurant to eat or into a store to shop.

5. In Polynesia, children take care of other children. This is not older kids temporarily babysitting younger siblings, but older children being formally in charge of raising younger children in the community.

6. Parents in Japan allow their young kids a lot of independence. Children as young as seven or even younger often ride the subway by themselves.

7. Spanish children typically don't go to bed until ten p.m. or later throughout childhood.

8. Among the Bayaka people in central Africa, there are no strictly defined male and female roles. Everyone hunts and cares for the children.

I'm not suggesting we should adopt all of these practices. I can promise you that most of these will *not* become staples in my household. I lived in New York City for nine years and as a frequent subway rider, it *terrifies* me to think of my kids taking the subway at age seven! We allowed Caroline to take the train into the city by herself at age twelve a few times, but I would drop her at the station, watch her walk onto the platform, and stay on the phone with her the whole time until my husband picked her up at Grand Central Terminal. And I required a proof-of-life photo to be sent. (I'm a little much. But it's also New York.)

These examples of parenting styles from other cultures peel back another layer. They move us out of our parenting echo chambers and introduce us to new ideas and ways of thinking.

They maybe even show us why other countries call us "intensive" parents and our kids "hot-housed."

If you feel like parenting in your house is an extreme sport, that's because it is. That's what we've made it. What we would post as #MomLife on our social media pages translates as #IntensiveParenting to the rest of the world. I don't particularly love this characterization; I'm defensive of America's working moms.

> If you feel like parenting in your house is an extreme sport, that's because it is. That's what we've made it.

I remember bringing Caroline home from the hospital. John drove up front, and I sat in the middle of the back seat beside our beautiful baby. As our car left the parking lot, it was like the pink cloud of bliss suddenly cleared. Caroline started screaming, rain poured down from the sky, and John wanted to know what we should do about dinner. There I was, mesh panties and soggy pad, throbbing from boobs to bottom, exhausted, and suddenly in charge of another human's life.

If they would have readmitted us, I would have *joyfully* returned to the drowsy, dim hospital room where nurses and doctors told me exactly what my daughter needed every hour on the hour. But they don't send home a checklist or guidebook when they discharge you from labor and delivery. John and I were on our own.

So what do we do? We look around and see what other parents are doing, we pick and choose what we like and dislike, and we adopt our own set of parenting values, habits, and beliefs. But what if we're trapped in this American vortex of parenting styles and it's just not working, but we all keep trying, because none of us are willing to just say uncle?

And guess what? Intensive parenting isn't making us happier. In fact, it's making us mentally unwell. In a much-referenced study done in 2012, 181 mothers with children ages 5 and under completed a survey.[9] The results showed that "intensive mothering beliefs correlated with several negative mental health outcomes." Yep, we're talking greater depression and stress. The study results can be summed up like this: Aspects of intensive mothering beliefs are harmful to women's mental health.

> Intensive parenting isn't making us happier. In fact, it's making us mentally unwell.

MOM GUILT IS AMERICAN

I'm friends with an incredibly talented mom of three, Liz For-
kin Bohannon. Liz is the founder of Sseko Designs and the
author of the book *Beginner's Pluck: Build Your Life of Purpose and
Impact Now.*

Sseko Designs is an ethical fashion brand that provides employment and educational opportunities for women in Uganda and
enables women to continue their education and become leaders in
their country, breaking the cycle of poverty. In other words, Liz is
a warrior who also wears angel wings.

I was having a conversation with Liz about this book, about
mom guilt, and here's what she said: "Mom guilt is an American
thing. We don't ask for help. We'd rather have our status as a martyr than the help of a tribe."

Liz isn't being callous in her assessment—she's being honest.
She goes on to discuss the paradigm of mom guilt in our country
as compared to the country of Uganda, where so much of her work
is centered. She said, "I think a fundamental part of the mom
guilt conversation, specifically as it relates to 'working mom versus
stay-at-home mom,' is that we acknowledge the inherent moun-
tain of privilege upon which this conversation sits. The vast majority of people in the world do not have the option."

Liz went on to discuss how women and men in most countries
must do everything they can—both paid and unpaid labor—in
order to meet the most basic needs of their children and family. "I
have significant experience living and working in a global context,
specifically in East Africa, where the concept of 'mom guilt' is as
foreign to them as matoke [a staple food in Uganda] was to me
when I first arrived."

And it isn't just because Ugandans lack many of the luxuries we enjoy as Americans that predicates our mom guilt. Liz explained that it's also because "our sisters and brothers across the world have a much more developed, rooted, and healthy concept and framework for interdependence and community. The bogus expectation that a mother can 'do it all' without asking for help is so much less prevalent in a global context. Dependence on one another is seen not as a weakness to be avoided at all cost, but as a value and fabric of a healthy community and society."

Liz described how the structure for the "nuclear family" is less rigid and more expansive in countries like Uganda. "Friends and extended family support one another in more integrated ways, and the fear of 'being a burden' is so much less prevalent."

This might be surprising, but paid domestic labor outside of the United States is much more socially accepted. "In the United States," Liz said, "there can be a lot of shame when women pay for domestic labor support. There is an underlying sense that she should be able to carry it all and needing support (paid or unpaid) is a signal that she is either failing to keep it all together or is somehow 'lazy' for 'farming out' work that inherently belongs to her." So the American woman "should" be able to do it all, and to hire help is to capitulate to her own shortcomings? Really?

"I've learned firsthand from communities across the global south that this isn't the global norm, but this healthier dynamic isn't limited to East Africa or developing economies. One of my best friends has lived in Paris for several years and was just sharing with me how much more common and acceptable (and affordable) domestic support is, and a belief that parents (moms especially) should have time and space to pursue their own health, their social lives, and their careers is not in opposition to being a good parent but is in fact part of the equation."

Liz doesn't discount how there are mamas across the globe who are exhausted and burned out from taking care of their kids. "Let us be very clear that there is…war, conflict, poverty, and genocide happening and that mothers globally are carrying extreme stress and weight as they do all they can to care for and protect their children. I do not believe that moms in America are worse off than many mothers across the globe. But here in America, there is a unique and unnecessary pressure and burnout that results from an idealization of independence and the impossible standards we hold women to work their jobs like they don't have children and raise children like they don't have a job. And we can be a part of changing that."

The American way of parenting, being a family, and distributing labor is not working, and it's not making us happy. So why do we keep doing it? What can we do to change it?

THE ECHO CHAMBER

Have you ever heard the term *echo chamber*? Before I tell you what it is, let's do another experiment together. Scroll through the list of people you follow on Instagram, Facebook, TikTok, Reddit, Twitter, blogs, or whatever social media platform you visit most.

Answer the following questions for the majority of the people on your list:

1. Are they from the same country as you?
2. Are they the same race as you?
3. Do they share the same spiritual beliefs as you?
4. Do they share similar political beliefs as you?
5. Do they share similar interests or hobbies as you?

An echo chamber is any environment in which a person encounters only those beliefs or opinions that coincide with their own. Their existing views are reinforced, and alternative ideas are not considered. Our social media platforms—which we now use as our main source for information to form our opinions—act as an echo chamber.

We think it's normal to live this way. We think this is what parenting is like—tiring, thankless, and endless. But our perception isn't normal. It's American. And it's reinforced every day when we get online and see other moms hacking it right alongside us. But there's a better way. A less-intensive way to parent. A way that doesn't give us clinical depression.

For one, we've got to take back our authority in our households. When our kids try to control the temperature of the house or when they try to exert their authority, we pause and say, "Hey. Who is the boss of this house?" They say, "You are." We say, "Who is the employee?" They say, "We are." It's stupid, but it resets the moment and reminds them they're not in charge.

Did you know that in France, there is no such thing as a kids' menu? Kids are taught to eat like adults from the moment they're able to eat solid foods. This has ensured that very few kids are picky eaters. They often sit at the table well behaved for long stretches of time, don't require snacking, and are open to trying a large variety of new foods.

In French, *Ferme la bouche* means "shut your mouth," and it's one of the few phrases I recall from my high school French class. Maybe it's because my teacher was constantly yelling this phrase at me. I'm a talker. Anyway, sounds like there's no need for this to be said over family dinners in France.

When it comes to dinnertime in my house, it's a losing battle.

Pickiness abounds. John and I have almost gotten divorced about 689 times because neither of us enjoy the kitchen. You know what? Every single one of my kids knows how to make a sandwich. Though, admittedly, none of them like the same kind of sandwich. My only job is to earn enough money to keep meat, cheese, peanut butter, and bread on the table. Instead of battling my husband and my mom guilt, I need to let my kids eat a dang ham and Swiss. Or one of the many Uncrustables PB&Js I always keep stocked.

We're big proponents of boundaries at work and boundaries with family members outside our house, but how about boundaries with our kids? *No* is a powerful word. We've all got to commit to saying it more.

Pamela Druckerman, a former reporter for the *Wall Street Journal*, moved to Paris after losing her job. She married a British expatriate and, not long after, gave birth to a daughter. She documented the experience of raising Bean, "the most ill-behaved child in every Paris restaurant," in her book *Bringing Up Bébé*.[10]

> We're big proponents of boundaries at work and boundaries with family members outside our house, but how about boundaries with our kids?

Pamela noticed the stark difference between the way her daughter behaved during public meals and the way French children could sit calmly through three entire courses. Bean was throwing food by the time the appetizers hit the table.

Pamela talked to a lot of French mothers, and here's what she learned: "French parents don't worry that they're going to damage their kids by frustrating them. To the contrary, they think their kids will be damaged if they can't cope with frustration."

One mother told Pamela that she always waited five minutes

before picking up her infant daughter when she cried. This same mother was explaining her parenting methods while her three-year-old was in the kitchen baking cupcakes. By herself.

Pamela's biggest takeaway? Just say *non*—and when French parents say it, they actually mean it. French parents view learning to cope with *no* as a crucial step in a child's developmental process. "It forces them to understand that there are other people in the world, with needs as powerful as their own."

This is a much more effective method than me telling my kids, "The world doesn't revolve around you!" in frustration.

> French parents view learning to cope with *no* as a crucial step in a child's developmental process.

MENTALLY TOUGH

We've also got to give our kids more credit when it comes to responsibility. We don't have to protect them from the big, bad world nearly as much as we feel the pressure to.

The year I turned forty-four, I suffered my third miscarriage. I already had three kids, but as the youngest of four, I always pictured myself with one more. After that many losses, you're really not surprised to see blood in your underwear. It's just as crushing, but not as shocking.

This miscarriage happened over Fourth of July weekend 2019. John and I had taken the kids to our friend's home in Maryland. While we were at a restaurant, I saw the spotting. The bleeding increased to the point that I was stuffing washcloths, paper towels, anything I could find in that restaurant bathroom into my underwear to stop the flow. But it just kept coming.

I made a decision then that I've caught a lot of heat for—a *lot*.

I brought my then twelve-year-old daughter, Caroline, into the bathroom with me. I explained to her what was going on and said, "I just want to let you know that the baby is probably no longer living. Mommy is sad but doesn't feel any guilt. This is normal; it happens to so many women. It's happened to me a couple of other times. When you get pregnant, it might happen to you, honey. And I want you to know there's nothing you did wrong."

I shared this experience on *The View*, and though I didn't expect everyone to agree with my choice, I gotta say, the backlash was mind-blowing. And telling. You would have thought that I showed Caroline a sex tape. Here is just a sampling of Facebook comments[11] from *People* magazine's page:

"This lady is not very smart."
("This lady" being me.)

"Too much drama for a 12-year-old."
(Twelve-year-olds know *nothing* about drama, right?)

"Kinda sick to do that."
(Would it have been less sick to pretend nothing happened?)

"Sorry for your loss but why traumatize your child just to endorse your weird feministic belief."
(If wanting to protect my daughter from the guilt and shame associated with miscarriages is being weirdly feministic, sign me up.)

"Why is she making this public? It says to me that she just wants some attention. I have no clue who she is."

(Yes, I do want some attention. I want some attention for the two in five women who will experience miscarriages in their lifetime and feel the heartache and shame that I have felt three times in my life. Also, hi! I'm Paula.)

No, I don't expect everyone to agree with all my choices as a parent, and we'll get to mom shaming in the next chapter. My point in sharing this story is that most of the pushback I received was based on the assumption that my twelve-year-old couldn't possibly emotionally process that I was having a miscarriage in real time.

Caroline's reaction? She's an empath. She wanted to be there for me. She hugged me and asked if she could bring me a glass of water. We both cried. She was grieving too—she had just lost a sibling. Allowing our kids to see our pain doesn't hurt them; it gives them permission to feel their own pain.

Our kids are far more mentally tough than we give them credit for. They live in a world of fifteen-second attention spans, sex sells, divorce as the norm, and,

> Allowing our kids to see our pain doesn't hurt them; it gives them permission to feel their own pain.

yes, a world filled with death and loss. I remember going to a funeral as young as four. My grandfather had passed, and I asked if I could look in his casket.

My dad told me I then asked if I could touch him and said he was cold. My parents explained to me that Gido was in heaven, and that what I was seeing in the casket was just his shell. When my daddy passed in 2019, I had that same conversation with my youngest. He kissed *his* gido on the cheek, gave him his stuffed animals, and now talks about seeing him again in heaven and wrestling him (this was how they connected).

Here's a dichotomy to consider.

We want our kids to play sports, join clubs, take all the advanced courses, apply to colleges, fly from our nests, and never return, right? That's the parenting "win." Nice, squeaky-clean kids who have never seen the sight of blood or heard the whisper of a profanity.

But do we also want our kids to experience the dark, painful, and shame-filled moments that life promises to bring on their own? With no example to follow after? We're supposed to politely sweep those stories under the rug? The bloody stories? The stories we don't share about on social media? The stories that make our cheeks flame with shame?

We're not supposed to share those because they may become "traumatized"?

Sorry. I don't buy it. We can't keep our feet in both worlds. We're raising kids who can perform but cannot perceive. Kids who can earn but can't empathize. Kids who can argue but can't face adversity.

> We're raising kids who can perform but cannot perceive. Kids who can earn but can't empathize. Kids who can argue but can't face adversity.

Please don't hear this as a lecture. That's the last thing working moms need, and we do a fantastic job of beating ourselves up all by ourselves. Hear this as a battle cry. We haven't been taught any better. We've been stuck in this echo chamber for far too long and we're *almost* too tired to crawl out. If you do anything for your kids, for yourself, use that last bit of supermom power I know you have and get out. Open your ears to the truth.

There is something better for you. For us. For our kids. And it's already happening.

I have some good news that should at the very least bring a little sunlight into the shadows of your mom guilt. A study done by Harvard University showed that daughters of working moms experience better careers, higher salaries, and more equal relationships than daughters of stay-at-home moms. The same study showed that sons of working moms were more likely to grow up to be great dads. "Adult sons of working mothers were also more likely to spend time caring for family members."[12]

Like a lot of things in parenting, how we're doing as moms is almost impossible to measure day to day. But the long-term data tells us that having a career doesn't marginalize our influence in our kids' lives. In fact, it does the opposite.

Let's make a commitment to avoid the sugar-coated bubble of propriety. Let's vow to say no. Let's vow to allow our kids to see us cry, see us hurt, see us betrayed, see us depressed, see us grieve—and then vow to give them a model to replicate that it is possible for them, too, to come back from the obstacles of life.

We have been hand-picked to raise the children in our care. We have what it takes to do it. Let's make one last vow: that we won't carry our kids through life without letting their feet get a little dirty.

> Let's make one last vow: that we won't carry our kids through life without letting their feet get a little dirty.

CHAPTER FIVE

CARRYING YOUR ID

Mom guilt is an American thing. We don't ask for help. We'd rather have our status as a martyr than the help of a tribe.

—Liz Bohannon, founder and mom of three

There isn't a polite way to say this, but my son Landon has always found it hilarious to smack people's butts. He thinks it's funny. Which it is—as long as it's not the butt of a stranger.

We were on vacation with my in-laws and parents, and we all went out to spend time by the pool. I decided to take Caroline and JJ on a walk by the beach. When we got back, John looked like he'd swallowed a beehive. My Spidey sense told me something was up.

"What's wrong?" I asked.

John relayed his tale of mortification.

Apparently, Landon had walked up to a woman, thinking she was me (she was wearing a black bathing suit that was similar to mine). He pulled back his hand as hard as he could and smacked her on the butt, giggling.

The woman turned around. "Wow," she said. "You're starting early!"

Luckily, she had a good sense of humor. My husband was beyond pale—basically translucent—by the time I walked up. He pointed her out to me. I was so embarrassed; I couldn't say anything to her. If by a miracle, you were on vacation at the Hard Rock Cafe in the Dominican Republic back in 2017, and a random, cute kid smacked you on the rear…this is the apology you deserved: I am so sorry.

This isn't the only case of mistaken identity I've experienced. This other one is only slightly less humiliating. If you've read *Called Out*, you know I went through seven months of absolute suffering in 2017. I had a miscarriage, a concussion, a head-on car crash, and influenza that turned into pneumonia. During this horrendous season, I didn't care what I looked like when I went out. I was unkempt and made no apologies about it.

I frequented a favorite Dunkin' Donuts in New Rochelle, New York, just down the road from my house, where I'd get my go-to: iced decaf coffee with toasted almond, half-and-half on the side. I went in so often that the gentleman who worked there became a familiar face. One day during my personal hell, I went in looking really, really rough—emphasis on *rough*.

I saw my Dunkin' employee and waved to him. I don't even know if I gave a fake smile or not, but I'm sure I tried. I could tell he was studying me. Finally, he said, "Do you have a younger sister who comes in here a lot?"

"No," I said. "That's actually me. When I don't look like hell."

Another mistaken identity.

Or there was the time I wasn't recognized at work by the security guard who had patted me down countless times on my way into the studio. Maybe it's because I showed up in my pajamas, holding a pillow. In my defense, I was rolling in around four a.m. to anchor *Good Morning America*, still half-asleep.

Our identities are complex. We base so much of who we are on what we do, how we perform, how others perceive us, and whether or not we're checking all the boxes on our imaginary "in order to be acceptable" lists. Because of this, working moms are constantly in a state of identity crisis. We think we should be able to carry it all, but it's impossible. So when the inevitable dropped ball hits the ground, our self-image shatters right next to it.

> Working moms are constantly in a state of identity crisis.

LOSE YOURSELF

When I worked at ABC, I was a journalist. That's who I was. I started in radio (after a quick stint at Arby's and several years of cleaning apartments) and then climbed my way up the ladder one painstaking step at a time. I had made it. I was anchoring one of the biggest morning shows in the world, and our ratings were soaring. I had given myself to my work—all of myself. My energy, my thoughts, my time. I exchanged me for my role.

My work had become my worth. My calling became singular: career. My value was my vocation. I was Paula Faris, co-anchor of *Good Morning America: Weekend Edition*, co-host of *The View*.

And when I chose to pump the brakes in 2018, when those

titles were gone, who was I? I was completely and utterly lost. The identity crisis came swiftly.

Fast-forward to two years later. When I left ABC in 2020, I went in the complete opposite direction for a bit. I decided to mom, and I mommed hard. We came to South Carolina and felt a peace about staying, and I settled in to being home full-time.

I still recall the conversation I had with my kids after our last caregiver left. Up until that point, we'd had either nannies or au pairs—a privilege, I admit. An au pair is something I hadn't even heard of until we moved to New York. They essentially are live-in nannies from foreign countries who are looking for a cultural and educational experience. And, by the way, I had no choice in childcare during this time in my career. I had to leave the house before four a.m. every morning, so daycare wasn't an option, and having a nanny was actually *more* expensive than having a live-in au pair.

Anyway, on that summer day in 2020, we'd just said goodbye to our final au pair and dropped her at the airport, and I remember asking my kids to give me some grace. This was the first time since I became a mama that I didn't have childcare—I needed to figure out how to be a mom without a safety net.

I was a little anxious about it, because I wasn't sure I could do it and, until that point, I hadn't done it.

During this time, I pretty much did a 180. I went from being gone a lot to taking my kids to school, picking them up from school, going to all of their events, being with them all the time.

I love, love, love being a mom.

The author Elizabeth Stone said it best: "Making the decision to have a child—it's momentous. It is to decide forever to have your heart go walking around outside your body."[1]

Momming is absolutely my favorite job. But I've also learned it's easy for us moms to pour all our identity into being a mom.

Because one day we're asked, "What do you like to do in your free time? What are your hobbies?" and we don't have an answer. We lose ourselves.

I lost myself at work. And then I lost myself at home.

I went from a hard-charging career to staying at home with equal tenacity and abandon.

> I lost myself at work. And then I lost myself at home.

The pendulum of my identity has swung from one side clear to the other. And guess what? I still don't feel like I'm nailing it. I still haven't found the elusive "balance." I'm still exhausted. Maybe it's because when we base our identity on the external, on the temporary roles we play in life, we're guaranteed a tailspin when those roles shift or disappear.

MOTHER MARTYR MENTALITY

A few years ago my daughter, Caroline (who is still in middle school as I'm writing this book), was talking about wanting to go on a bike excursion called Bike Across America. "It would look great on a college application," she said.

"That's great, honey!" I said encouragingly, proud of my independent, forward-thinking daughter.

Just kidding. I actually burst into tears. I get choked up when I get emails about her going to high school. I'll think, *I wish she'd just go. Just leave me and get it over with.* How ridiculous is that? The thought of her applying to colleges? I don't feel ready. And don't even get me started on my youngest leaving home to pursue life on his own. My brain refuses to compute that reality.

I know I'm not alone. Jennie Allen is a podcaster, *New York Times* best-selling author, and mom of four. I interviewed her about this exact topic. "Do you want me to get real here?" Jennie said. "My identity has gotten more tied up into motherhood than it has my job. I went through such a season of grief when my first-born left for college. I spun out. I just did not know what to do. And I had all these fears that my kids were just gonna go and leave me. And all this investment I've put in for most of my life wasn't going to matter anymore. It was just for nothing."

I think we all play emotional tug-of-war between the ideas of empowering our kids to take the next steps in life and the idea that they will reach the next steps in life and leave us at the bottom of the staircase. Maybe I'm projecting some of my own guilt here. I left Jackson, Michigan, after I graduated in 1993, and I never returned.

I love Michigan and always identify as a Midwestern kid. I am so proud of my roots. But there's never really been an opportunity to return to Michigan. Living in Chicago between 2005 and 2011 was the closest I came—roughly four hours from my hometown. I wish I had been closer to my parents. Caroline, JJ, and Land-o: If you leave South Carolina and never come back, I will find you!

I see my own bittersweet pain echoed in the hearts of moms everywhere, especially over social media. "Let them be little" and "Time, slow down!" are familiar phrases we throw out or hashtag, along with "The days are long, the years are short." I think if you peel back the layers of this sentiment, there's a lot of fear underneath. And it's not the fear that our children will leave the nest and fail, it's that once our kids leave the nest, they won't need us anymore. *I feel this so deeply.*

I'll often look through their baby photos and listen to tear-inducing music that tortures my mommy heart until I'm a mess. It's usually "Sunrise, Sunset" from *Fiddler on the Roof* or "A Thousand Years" by Christina Perri. I need to be needed by my kids. And for those of us who have based too much of our identity on motherhood, the idea that they may spread their wings and fly the coop to never return is an arrow through our heart.

If we're not mothers running ragged in the carpool line, then who are we? We think the only thing we have to offer the world is our ability to parent, but that's not true. We've been created to play a dynamic role in this world. We've got skills and gifts and talents that can be utilized outside the walls of our homes. The investment we make in our families is our greatest investment, but it's not the only investment we're capable of.

> We think the only thing we have to offer the world is our ability to parent, but that's not true. We've been created to play a dynamic role in this world.

If we base our value on any one thing or role, we're sure to be disappointed or hurt or to experience rejection as the seasons of life rage on. This is also where we get into a bit of trouble with having a "mother martyr" mentality. We sacrifice ourselves at the altar of being a mom. We give up our dreams. We give up our comfort. We give up our appearance. Why? Because we think it makes us a better mother? I've found no science to support that carrying the mother martyr ID improves our kids' lives, our lives, or our family as a whole. In fact, I've found the opposite.

MODERN-DAY "BOSS BABES"

When my dad passed away, I was driving home from the funeral with my mom. She looked at me and said, "Paula, I've been your father's wife for fifty-three years. I don't know what I'm supposed to do now."

I could see that she looked lost, and it absolutely crushed me. I wondered what my mom's life would have been like if she'd had the same choices I had. I asked my mom what other roles she had dreamed of playing in her life but hadn't had the chance to. "After high school, I wanted to do something noble, like join the Peace Corps," Mom said. "I signed up for it, but wasn't able to participate because my dad fell on hard times. He got laid off, and I needed to work to help support my family."

My mom's first job was at the dime store when she turned fourteen. She earned sixty-five cents an hour to contribute to the household bills. When I asked her if she felt like she missed out on the opportunity to live *her* version of her life, she said, "No, that's just how we lived."

My mom was raised in a Catholic home, which was a motivating factor in many of the decisions she made as a mother. For many growing up in the Christian faith, there are very "traditional" expectations about what being a "good Christian woman" is supposed to look like. I felt some of these perceived restrictions and tensions in my own career journey.

Maybe you're not a person of faith, and this is one of the reasons why. You had no interest in conforming to the mold of a meek, submissive, and docile housewife, so you rejected Christianity. Speaking as a follower of Christ, I get it. There's no judgment.

The church at large has tossed some heavy things onto the load we carry as working moms. I reached out to Lysa TerKeurst, who founded Proverbs 31 Ministries back in 1992, and her director of theology and research, Joel Muddamalle. I asked them some tough questions about what the Bible really says about women. Their comments were very freeing for me, as someone who's struggled with working outside the home.

"When people would say things like, 'Aren't you worried what you spending time at work will do to your kids?' it was a gut punch," Lysa told me.

"The Bible has a lot to say about women and work," Joel said. "In fact, the opening pages of Scripture place Adam (man) and Eve (woman) together in a Garden, and are both told to 'subdue' the earth and 'rule/have dominion' over the fish, birds, and every living thing on earth" (Genesis 1:26–28).

Joel explained how vitally important this precedent is to the discussion of women and vocation, because it models that the established pattern for humanity (men and women) was laboring together. In other words, there is no indication that one gender was left behind to "take care of things" while the other was to go out and subdue.

The historical lives of three women support his position, Joel told me. First is Deborah, who is discussed in the book of Judges, chapters 4 and 5.[2] "Deborah serves as a prime example of a woman in the Old Testament who had a vocation outside of the home. She is introduced as a prophetess, a title of an official position within the Israelite community, and then her actions are celebrated in Judges 5 through a song. Of all the judges in the book of Judges, only Deborah is ever seen acting in an official capacity judging, or handling the civil issues of the community as she sits at Deborah's Palm tree [Judges 4:4–5], an activity that was well known and associated with the official act of passing judgment."

Deborah has a title and position in the Israeli culture, but the Bible also points out that a man named Barak refused to go out to battle unless Deborah joined him. The Bible is known for its metaphorical language, but as Joel points out, this isn't that. "Clearly, this means that Deborah must leave her home and her family in order to go out to war [Judges 4:8]. In this turn of events, we find that Deborah is not only a prophetess who speaks the Word of God to the people of God, but she is also a judge in a civil sense, at the tree, *and* in a militaristic sense as she goes out to battle."

I would like to think that Deborah and I would have gotten along, but honestly, this lady sounds badass on a whole other level. I'm not easily intimidated, but a prophet, judge, *and* soldier? Deborah, you may be my hero.

Joel also pointed out Huldah, whose story we read in 2 Kings 22:14–20. Similar to Deborah, Huldah is called a prophetess in 2 Kings 22:14 and plays a crucial role in relaying the message of God to King Josiah. This leads us to believe that she was well respected in the royal palace.[3]

And then there's the Proverbs 31 woman...

I'd just like to say, what Joel and Lysa had to say about her might blow your mind like it did mine.

"I've always found it odd that when having conversations about the Proverbs 31 woman in the Bible, some people seem to hyperfocus on her roles in the home," Lysa said. "She was absolutely responsible in her roles as a wife and mother. And she was also a stellar businesswoman who fulfilled important roles outside of the home."

"For too long we have relegated the Proverbs 31 woman to the household in a domestic sense," Joel added. "To take care of the children, wash the dishes, clean the house, and, if necessary, do some small work within the household that may help financially. But this last part has been frowned upon."

Why?

"Maybe because we have been disconnected from the ancient Near Eastern context of the woman who is described in Proverbs 31," said Joel. "The women in the ancient world were much more than homemakers; they were the source of stability, security, and strength for the home internally *and* externally. In a culture where men were often out to war, the women were responsible not only for the care of their families, but for the household business that made it possible for the family to survive. This paints a drastically different picture of the Proverbs 31 woman. The woman described in Proverbs 31 had exclusive responsibility for her household and beyond her house to manage the lands that were owned by the family [Proverbs 31:16]. She went into the market regularly to handle business negotiations and trade [Proverbs 31:18, 24]."

The wealth that came into the household here is different from the dowry a woman would bring to a marriage. In the context of Proverbs 31, the accumulation of wealth is a result of economic growth that comes from her shrewd dealings in the market. In other words, the Proverbs 31 woman is the ancient version of a modern-day "boss babe."

BADASS WOMEN OF THE BIBLE

- The Proverbs 31 woman: "She considers a field and buys it; out of her *earnings* she plants a vineyard. She sets about her work vigorously; her arms are strong for her tasks" (Proverbs 31:16–17).

- Sheerah, mentioned in 1 Chronicles 7:24, who built three towns: She "built Lower and Upper Beth Horon as well as Uzzen Sheerah."

- Those shepherds the angels appeared to on the night of Christ's birth: According to my friend Tara-Leigh Cobble, author of *The Bible Recap*, some scholars believe those shepherds were likely women—just another way Renaissance paintings may have misled us. Shepherding wasn't an uncommon job for a woman.

DIVIDING TASKS AND
RESPONSIBILITIES EQUALLY

If you grew up in a conservative Christian home or church, these examples may sound a bit "off" to you. You may remember bits and pieces of these women's stories, but you may be pleasantly surprised or impressed by others. Why isn't more said from the lecterns and pulpits about the work of these powerful and notable women? I don't know. But I have a hunch.

Let's review the remainder of Joel's research before we come to a conclusion. But I've got to tell you, it's getting hot under this University of Michigan hoodie I'm wearing.

So, what about the New Testament? Is this where the cultural shift takes place? Is this where God tells women to sit down, shut up, mind their kids, and get back in the kitchen? Nope.

Take the story of Mary and her sister, Martha, for example. It is a Christian favorite. Jesus and a few other disciples are at their house for a visit. Martha's running around like a chicken with her head cut off, preparing the food, doing the dishes—you know, the hostess stuff us women can get a little carried away with.

What's her sister doing? Sitting at Jesus' feet with the rest of Jesus' followers, learning.

Why was Mary so comfortable taking her spot as a pupil of Jesus? Shouldn't she have been in the kitchen with Martha? The answer may be simple. Maybe she was just familiar with Jesus. They were friends. But it's clear Mary felt welcome to join the men in the room as a student and a scholar.

Joel points out: "Remember, Mary is in mixed company, as the disciples were men. This is an incredibly powerful scene where Jesus accepts Mary at His feet, as one of His disciples, and therefore, Jesus—as all rabbis would—has expectations that His disciples would not be perpetual students, but would one day be teachers, and Mary is included."

In Acts 18:26 we meet Priscilla. Priscilla not only is a teacher but also owns the home where the church meets and is its patron. "In the Greco-Roman world, a patron of the household was not a housekeeper, cleaning dishes, making food, and being hospitable. Sure, it may have been included, but a patron in the Greco-Roman context was a leader of the household bringing order and even authority to the house and all those that were part of the house. The patron was held liable for all things that went on in the house."

There's another New Testament woman named Phoebe who

held a position in her church's leadership. "In Romans 16:1, Paul chooses her to deliver what may be the most important letter to the church in Rome." Phoebe was a courier. That may not sound like a particularly prestigious role, but in her day, it was. "In the Greco-Roman world, this would be a person that not only reads the letter, but is also responsible to teach and explain its nuances and answer. Remember, if the people had a question about the letter, they couldn't jump on FaceTime with Paul to clarify." No, that was the courier's job. To read the letter, understand it, deliver it, and then explain it. In a time when letters were the most powerful and direct form of communication, Phoebe's role was crucial to the establishment of the early church.

"So much more can and should be said about women and their importance in every aspect of life including family, the workplace, and ministry," Joel continues. "We could talk about Junia, a woman who was called an apostle by Paul in Romans 16:7. We could mention Euodia and Syntyche from Philippians 4:2, who were probably merchants based on their names, like another wealthy woman, Lydia, who is referenced in Acts 16:14–15."

So when we trace back God's design for the role of women in the workplace, the evidence shows that his original intent was not just to include women in the labor force, but to divide tasks and responsibilities equally between Adam and Eve. We see examples of this division of work throughout the Old and New Testament, with female judges, temple workers, trusted advisers, scholars, and couriers.

As Joel concludes, "The evidence that we have explored shows good reason, rationale, and permission for women to work outside the home and embrace their God-given ambition to the good of humanity and the glory of God."

Lysa adds, "I think instead of us spending energy debating what's the right place for a woman, why not give her grace to seek the Lord, get wise counsel, and determine her calling in each season of her life? Take a deep breath. Keep evaluating with honest eyes and an open heart. You probably won't get this all right. But if you keep your priorities in check, you'll be exactly where you're supposed to be. And always remember, one of the best gifts a mom can give her kids is the best version herself."

GRAPPLING WITH QUESTIONS

Is this the experience of women in the church today? Hardly. My alma mater, Cedarville University, has taken some pretty drastic stances on the role of women in church and society—it's why I refused to speak when I was asked to many years ago.

The president of the university had called me and personally asked me to speak on campus. He knew my story, how I'd climbed the ranks of broadcasting with a supportive partner by my side. When I asked him if he'd have done for his wife what John did for me, to sacrifice some of his own career ambitions for a time to support his wife's, he said no, and that, frankly, he didn't agree with it from a biblical perspective.

I quickly realized the only reason I was being asked to speak was so the university could take credit for my perceived success. I was going to be a pawn. No, thank you. Especially if you don't support the way it happened.

Until you're comfortable with someone like Joyce Meyer speaking on campus, until you're comfortable with women being allowed to preach, I won't be back. And it truly pains me to say that.

I absolutely loved my time at Cedarville—I got a great

education, felt incredibly supported by my broadcasting professors, made lifelong friends, plus I met John there. But I'm disappointed by the recent direction of the university, which stems from its leadership. Misogyny isn't a good look, especially when it's veiled in Christianity.

Too often, that's exactly what Christianity is—misogyny in disguise. It's an excuse to diminish women, to "put us in our place," to get us to submit. That didn't sit well with Jesus, and it certainly shouldn't sit well with us.

Look, this section has been really hard for me to write. I don't love calling out Christianity or my alma mater. It saddens me. Why? Because Jesus is the bedrock of my life. But what I hope is that these truths about how God actually views women can provide freedom for many and ultimately shine a light on how pivotal women were and remain to Jesus' ministry.

If you're a Christian, you know we're often asked to ground our identity in our faith. But if our faith tells us our identities set us in the background of the church's ministry, what message does that send about our value? Our gifts? Our abilities to contribute? And how in the world did we get here?

Beth Allison Barr is a medieval history professor at Baylor University who studies the role of women in evangelical Christianity. Beth is also a devout Christian and a working mom. In her book *The Making of Biblical Womanhood: How the Subjugation of Women Became Gospel Truth*, she uses historical analysis to challenge contemporary claims of Scriptural gender roles.

Writing in the *New Yorker*, Eliza Griswold says, "Barr's book argues that the modern version of [gender roles] was invented in the twentieth century, in response to an increasingly effective feminist movement, to reinforce cultural gender divisions. 'Women think all of this is the Bible because they learn it in their churches…But it's really a post–Second World War construction of domesticity, which was designed to send working women back to the kitchen."[4]

That's right. We're back to the destructive curse of the 1950s housewife—a notion so influential, apparently, that it reached into our churches and into our faith and caused us to question our identities at their deepest level.

My mom is clearly not the only woman who has grappled with these questions. I have too. I've wrestled with guilt and shame over my own callings that for years took me out of the home and out of the homemaker role I mistakenly believed my faith called women and mothers to take.

Maybe you're not a Christian, but your culture or faith has instilled similar standards and expectations for a woman's role in the family. Maybe you, too, have struggled with your identity, because what your faith or your culture tells you contradicts your wiring. You're not alone.

I'd encourage you to do the same type of research. Maybe even take a personal inventory. Peel back the layers to see what's underneath those customs and practices. Ask yourself why those habits exist. Question whether or not they serve you as a human being, mother, worker, and woman.

IDENTITY ISSUES

A mom I know, who I'll call Stephanie, her husband, and their three daughters moved from the United States to Spain in 2014 as missionaries. When I reached out to Stephanie to ask if she'd noticed a difference between the working moms in Spain and the working moms in the States, here's what she said: "There is a saying in Spain and other countries in Europe: 'Europeans work to live; Americans live to work.' The expectation in the United States is a long to-do list, productivity, and running ourselves ragged. In Spain, people only work to have enough funds to enjoy their life. People rent houses more than they own, accumulate less stuff (I haven't been to any Pinterest-worthy houses), and value time and travel more than getting their identity wrapped up in their work."

She even joked, "I'm back in the States while we're getting my daughter set up in college. I'm doing some contract work for a friend. I wonder what he'll think about my new work ethic (that I say no firmly and often). He may just think I'm lazy, but that's fine with me. I don't find my identity in my work now, which is the opposite of how I identified as a working mom in America."

The thought of being seen as lazy in work feels like a hand at my throat. Why is that? Because so much of my identity is wrapped up in being a hard worker. Can a hard worker say no? Can a hard worker have boundaries, like no emails or calls on the weekends? I want to say yes, but my work history says no. It says I still have a long way to go when it comes to developing a well-rounded, healthy identity as a working mom.

I recently had lunch with my friend Melanie. Melanie is brilliant. She taught middle school for many years, even after the passing of her first husband. In the last few years, Melanie has remarried and become a mother in her forties, and she struggled to carry it all. So she decided to take a step back and leave her role in education to focus on her home and kids. When we met, I could tell Melanie was conflicted by her decision.

I asked her, "What holds the biggest tension for you?"

Melanie didn't have to think. "Mom guilt for keeping my daughter in daycare even though I'm at home," she responded immediately. Then she added, "And wondering if other moms judge me for that. Guilt for still having the desire to want to work and volunteer outside the home in some capacity."

I understood that guilt—the guilt of ambition.

I asked Melanie what she feared. "When I left teaching after fifteen years, I wondered if I would still be important," she said. "Would I still have a place in our community as one who added value? I've worked since I was fourteen, so not working felt very strange to me, and still does at times. I want to savor this season and be fully present with my family. Will anyone find me valuable after this? Will I feel valuable?"

The off-ramps and on-ramps in and out of the workforce are brutal passages for women. We've already talked about the potential effects of a resume gap. But I also think we back ourselves into a corner, label ourselves, and think, *I have to do this one thing.* And so many of my colleagues and so many women in my circle have felt that if they dip out for a little bit, if they step away from the workforce, they won't be able to get back in. And so then they stay and feel trapped, or they decide to dip and focus on motherhood and then think, *Wow, there's no value in this because I got all of my value at work.* So it's a constant struggle of truly digging in and finding your identity.

I'm incredibly passionate about releasing women from the pressure of thinking you have to do one thing for the rest of your life.

Our best shot at changing things for the generation of working moms that will follow us is by making sure they're carrying the right

> I'm incredibly passionate about releasing women from the pressure of thinking you have to do one thing for the rest of your life.

ID—grounding their identity in what matters most. Not what you do, but who you are.

I want the generation behind me to know that what makes them unique are their talents and gifts, not what they're going to do when they grow up. "What do you want to do when you grow up?" is such a loaded question to ask kids. We're implying their job is going to be their contribution to society. I mean, we get the same question as adults. When you meet someone for the first time, they typically ask you two questions, in order: "What's your name?" and "What do you do?"

I believe we need to turn this question on its head. So much so that I wrote a children's book about it called *Who Do You Want to Be When You Grow Up?* It's releasing in 2023! A decade ago, I wouldn't have dreamed of writing a children's book. But here I am. Your professional evolution comes far easier when you understand that what you do is not who you are and vice versa.

What we are created to do will change throughout our lives, but who we are created to be will not. Let *that* be the ID that we carry. The others were never meant to be ours anyway.

CHAPTER SIX

CARRYING SUPERPOWERS

Moms are superheroes, and I'm honored to work with so many. I agree, finding more ways that allow them to be both supermom and super at work will be killer.

—Jon Zacharias, co-founder of GRO SEO Agency

Not very long ago, I had ten minutes to make JJ dinner, take a shower, and get him to practice. So what did I do? I strategized. I tossed some chicken on the grill. I knew I had five minutes before it needed to be flipped, so I hopped in the shower and washed all the necessary body parts (you know the ones, ladies), toweled off, and threw on my overalls. I brushed the tangles from my hair while I browned the other side of the chicken. I yelled for JJ to get in the car, sliced up the chicken, threw it in a container, and hopped in the car after him.

Done and *done*. Wonder Woman has *nothing* on the super-powers of a working mom. And it's worth mentioning that I do *not* envy her costume. It's like a strapless bathing suit and faux leather boots. I want to see a woman in yoga pants and a beat-up sweat-shirt fighting evil. Now *that's* a story I can get behind. She could even do it in blinged-out Golden Goose shoes.

Ready for another experiment? Put a mental checkmark (or an actual checkmark, if you're a write-in-the-book kind of woman) beside any of these statements that are true for you:

- I have nursed a baby or pumped breastmilk on a Zoom meeting.
- I have put on a full face of makeup with a child attached to me.
- I have answered work emails in the car rider line.
- I have taken a Zoom meeting in my car while waiting on a kid to come out of practice or club.
- I have gone to the bathroom with a child on my lap.
- I have put on makeup on the way to an event, function, or meeting.
- I have cooked a meal and also
    1. Gotten some part of my person dressed or
    2. Had a crying child hanging off one of my limbs or
    3. All of the above

If you answered yes to one or more of those questions, you are a superhero. You've got superpowers. You can accomplish multiple things at once—meaningful, important, must-do things. This is the intrinsic value of a working mom: She gets shit done, no matter the cost. And not only does she get shit done, but she gets it done well. My mom knows this is my mantra. As she says—because she won't say the s-word—"Paula, you GSD." LOL. I love you, Mom.

A CASE FOR THE WORKING MOM

In 2019 *Forbes* put out an article on how women-led companies compare to men-led companies. I'll be honest, when I started the article, I wasn't sure how the results would pan out. I hoped they'd at least fare equally well. I was wrong—but in a good way.

Women-led companies tend to perform better than those led by men.[1]

In an interview with ABC's *Shark Tank* investor Kevin O'Leary, Kevin confirms this assertion. "I've been investing now for over ten years on things like 'Shark Tanks' deals—and other deals that are brought to be because of 'Shark Tank'—and the majority of my returns come from the companies run by women," he said. "Now this isn't some kind of academic research, this is real data. This is real money coming back to me."[2]

Kevin points to his investment in Wicked Good Cupcakes, a company founded by mother-daughter duo Tracey Noonan and Danielle Vilagie. Why did Tracey and Dani start the company? They'd taken cake-decorating classes together as a way for Tracey, a working mom, to spend more quality time with her daughter, Danielle…and the rest is history.[3] Yep, talk about multitasking—they're now self-made millionaires with the top-selling cupcake in the world.

Out of the more than forty companies Kevin O'Leary has invested in, about 95 percent of the women-led companies met their financial targets, compared to just 65 percent for businesses with male leaders.[4]

Berlin Cameron, a boutique creative agency, recently developed a new division called Girl Brands Do It Better, which recently teamed up with the Harris Poll to do research on female-led organizations in our country. The results? Half of Americans would prefer to work for a woman-led company over a man-led company, including 46 percent of men. The same study revealed that 71 percent of both men and women feel that "having a woman in a leadership position makes them believe that they too can achieve a leadership position."[5]

We're not building a case against men. We're simply building a case for the working mom.

So, if women-led companies perform well and people want to work for them, why aren't women better represented in high-level management and leadership positions?

There's science behind the value of a working mom too.

A 2014 study done by the Federal Reserve Bank of St. Louis set out to measure the output of a working mom's career.[6] Since it's basically impossible to track the number of projects taken by a project manager, surgeries performed by a doctor, or cases taken by an attorney, the study developed a unique strategy for gathering data—it analyzed the number of published materials by more than ten thousand women in academia. If you've ever heard a college professor complain about having to publish, this method makes a ton of sense. In that world, publishing is *the* standard for work product.

Guess what they found? Over the course of a thirty-year career, mothers outperformed women without children in almost every year of being a working mom. Not only that, but moms with at least two kids were the most productive of all. "Using their own method for analyzing research publications, the authors found that within the first five or so years of their career, women who never have children substantially underperform those who do."[7]

While we're stating the facts, I am happy to report that working dads did well too. "For men, fathers of one child and those without children performed similarly throughout much of their careers. But men with two or more kids were more productive than both groups."

Why? Being a working parent makes you a better employee. And according to the studies and science, being a mom makes you the *best* employee. And yet research shows that resumes of non-mothers receive more than two times the callbacks of mothers.[8] I feel like we should all take a moment to pause here, maybe go outside and find a rooftop to scream this from: "Hey, corporate America! Moms are *not* your greatest liability! We are your greatest assets!"

To get ahead of any criticism, I'll admit that I've already heard some of it. During CARRY Media's press tour in May 2021, I went on a slew of TV shows—from *Good Morning America* to *Fox & Friends* and *The View*. After my appearance on *The View*, a few people said it felt like I was pitting women against one another by saying becoming a mother makes you smarter. What they heard was this: Moms are smarter than women without children. But let me say this: That's not my intent at all.

I realize someone will always be offended. However, I also understand how this section of the book might be interpreted. But when you've been part of a group that has been marginalized, deemed a risk or liability by the workforce, or told to "stay in the kitchen" where she belongs, you better believe I'm going to talk about the science that says moms have been typecast and how becoming a mom (and parent) expands your capacity—

you become more empathetic, efficient, a better leader, visionary, with increased courage. All that data I've already pointed you to? It's only reinforced by McKinney's "Strengthen the Mom-Force Survey" from April 2022, which says that 81 percent of moms say that being a mother has given them increased efficiency at work.[9]

Moms, stop apologizing. You're freaking baddies.

Here are a few reasons why moms needs to know their worth.

- Moms have been scientifically shown to become smarter and more empathetic during pregnancy.
- Parenting grows our emotional IQ, courage, efficiency/productivity, collaboration abilities, and compassion.
- Parents are extremely loyal to their employees when taken care of.
- Women-led companies are more profitable.
- The majority of employees want to work for women-led companies.

Leslie Forde is the co-founder of Mom's Hierarchy of Needs, an organization geared toward supporting the mental and emotional wellness of moms by creating safe spaces for parents to process their stress, dream big dreams, and live in possibility. "Parents get really good at context switching and exercising cognitive flexibility," Leslie explains, "which were both really crucial to being successful as leaders and as innovators. Parents are also a large part of the consumer space that organizations are often trying to serve. I spent most of my career in marketing, and organizations tend to forget this. The perspective and experience parents provide is an important one to have reflected on your internal teams in ways that match the goals you have for visibility in the external marketplace."

Parenthood is essentially a master class for leadership, empathy, vision, and efficiency. Getting my kids out the door for school? That's like being a hostage negotiator. Being in charge of another human is a monumental responsibility. It doesn't ever stop. It's an around-the-clock, forever-and-ever kind of commitment. It's a commitment that changes you. Being a parent develops muscles (figurative and literal) that you didn't even know you had.

THE "MOTHERHOOD PENALTY"

I saw something floating around on social media back in 2021, and for the life of me, I can't find it now. But here's the gist: A woman who had been out of the workforce for roughly five years to be more present with her children was applying for a job. The consensus was that she was extremely qualified. However, there was a major concern that she'd been out of the workforce for too long. So, they passed on her. It's called the "mommy gap."

I get *so fired up* about it.

This is why so many moms don't take the off-ramp when they want to or even need to—because there's the struggle and stigma to deal with when they want to get back in.

Can we just park here for a second? This woman is home, taking care of children, managing a household, multitasking like a boss, developing leadership skills that employers want in an employee, and becoming a higher-capacity employee than she was before she had kids, and now you're punishing her?

This makes *zero* sense.

A friend of mine texted me something the other day that angered me. It should anger you too.

She wrote: "Paula, I'm interviewing after five years on the sidelines. Haven't mentioned the word *family* once for fear of the mom penalty. Feels like I'm hiding the thing I'm proudest of."

For the sake of anonymity, I'll refer to her as Sarah. She's an experienced graphic designer, but she took some time off to raise her four children.

The "motherhood penalty" isn't just something that we've made up in our overworked, overtired minds. It's not conjecture. It's not anecdotal. And it's definitely not an anomaly. Sadly, it's a real thing where managers are less likely to hire mothers than women who don't have kids, and when they do hire a mother, they offer her a lower salary. But the real kick in the yoga pants? Men enjoy the converse "fatherhood bonus," where they are *more* likely to be hired than men without kids and are better compensated after becoming a parent.

To reiterate, moms aren't hired as often, we're paid less, and we're penalized for taking time away. We're treated as a flight risk—a liability.

Oh, she's a mom. She's been out of the workforce, probably counting Cheerios and singing nursery rhymes. She may skip meetings on occasion to care for sick kids. Moms have divided interests.

Employers aren't saying these things out loud, but they are thinking them.

But, in reality, there's *no* greater employee than a mother.

I'm often asked when I'm getting "back to TV." It flatters me on one hand, but it's also frustrating. I'm trying to give myself permission to do something different, trying to lean into momming as hard as I can, and be an independent contractor. It's not considered to be as "valuable" as what I was doing before—though I don't feel that way at all. I feel more fulfilled and my life feels more balanced than ever (although my bank account doesn't necessarily feel that way). I'm annoyed that many people still wrap my entire worth around my former job.

And then there are the unintentional scare tactics. I've had agents tell me the longer I remain a "former" *GMA* host, the more difficult it will be to "come back."

I'm not trying to go back to anything. I'm about moving forward. Why can't corporate culture just value where I am right now? I'm not any less of a hard worker. Let me choose my chapters. Sadly, women are punished for leaving the workforce to focus on mothering. But mothering is the most difficult work of all. It requires complete focus, meticulous planning, calendaring, systems, and so on. We aren't just sitting around counting Cheerios. We're gaining meaningful skills.

I should put on my resume: "2020–present: CEO of household, CFO of household, Events Manager, Uber Driver, Freelance Nurse, Arbitrator, Personal Assistant, Problem-Solver…"

I could honestly keep that list going, but I'll step off my soapbox now. I can't promise I won't return to this topic, because it irks me so much.

SCIENTIFIC SUPERPOWERS

Adam Franssen is a biology professor at Longwood University. He teamed up with other researchers, like Craig Kinsley of the University of Richmond, to prove his theory that being a mother makes a woman smarter. His findings? "Mothers are better at problem solving, handling stress and at completing certain memory tasks."[10]

But it's way more fascinating than that. Adam compares the brain of a pregnant woman to a car engine when it's revving:

> At the revving stage, a racecar's engine is getting prepped for that race. It seems like there is a lot of evidence to suggest that is actually what's happening in the mother's brain during the period of pregnancy. There are changes happening to neurons. They are increasing in size or some neurons have been shown to not only grow but to potentially increase their capacity to produce protein in one part of the brain or perhaps increase their neuronal branches to make communications from one neuron to another neuron that it wasn't talking with before—all in anticipation of the high workload of caring for a child.[11]

There goes the argument that a working mom's superpowers are learned behaviors. (If that's even an argument against them—learned behaviors are still behaviors with real results.) But isn't that incredible? It's wild, right? Moms' brains actually grow and increase in thinking capacity, even before our babies are born, because our bodies know the circus of newborn life…and toddler life…and tween life…and basically just how intense parenting is forever and ever and ever, amen.

A mother's brain maintains this heightened capacity throughout the remainder of her life. So when I said you're now carrying superpowers, I meant it. You are an evolutionary wonder!

And believe it or not, there's more to us than our big, brilliant minds. Just a few of the scientific superpowers being a mom gives us are time management mastery, empathy (self-awareness, psychological safety), and problem-solving and innovation skills.

Time Management Mastery

If you're a working mom, you know that life rises and falls on a solid family calendar—a calendar that almost always falls to the mom. Even in my busiest seasons, I was the birthday gift buyer, the party planner, the meal planner, the calendar manager, and the whose-family-are-we-visiting-for-the-holidays decider. If you're a single mom, there's still a mutual calendar to manage, and my bet is that you're the one doing the juggling.

I know exactly how many minutes it takes me to shower, get dressed, and get my three kids in the car. I know I can usually be ten minutes late to pick up from volleyball practice because they always go about ten later than planned. I know the best times to go grocery shopping, or if I've waited till the last minute (again) I'll order delivery (I've been rejoicing because DoorDash recently started delivering to my rural neighborhood). I know the rhythm of my household. I know when it's off. I just *know*. Time management isn't just a skill, it's an instinct.

When I was covering the wedding of Prince Harry to Meghan Markle in London back in 2018, I remember getting texts about school pickup and coordinating playdates with other moms while I was in London…literally on another continent. Planning child's play is *not* child's play. But I got it all done while doing the job I was assigned to do with flying colors.

As Craig H. Kinsley and Adam Franssen explain, in a mother's hippocampus, "neurons are undergoing changes of another sort, leading to increases in the concentration of tiny projections on the surface of dendrites, called dendritic spines."[12] Layman's language:

The hippocampus is the area of the brain that controls learning and memory. Craig and Adam's research proves what every working mom knows: We've got to remember everything—all of it.

> Practice schedules.
> That important Zoom meeting.
> The dentist appointment.
> When to upload our podcast.
> When the deadline to order yearbooks is (which reminds me—I forgot to order!).
> What time our therapist call is.
> When to put dinner in the slow cooker.

We've got to fit so many details into our brains that it is completely necessary for our mental capacity to expand.

Empathy

Sonogram pictures are creepy. You may disagree, but I'm blown away that technology hasn't advanced to a point where these images aren't so skeleton-y. I know you can get 3-D images taken once you're further along, but I'm talking about that out-of-the-gate strip of film that we plaster all over social media as if *our* baby looks any different from everyone else's.

When I found out I was pregnant with Caroline, I stared at the little gummy bear photo as if it were a Monet masterpiece. One day I was standing in the kitchen, holding the sonogram in complete wonder that this life was growing inside me. I started to cry. Not just a polite, sentimental cry. This was a violent sob. John walked in, raised his eyebrows in momentary concern, and then stepped right back out.

I'm sure you can relate. But there's actually a scientific reason we become more emotional during pregnancy—we're growing our empathy in order to make space for the new love we'll experience for our child. I remember holding Caroline when she was an infant and thinking, *My chest is going to explode. I can't handle how much I love this baby.* It's almost scary, isn't it, to be so inextricably connected to a human you know you can't hold in your arms forever?

The truth is, becoming a mother opens up emotional floodgates that you didn't know were dammed up inside of you. You experience the world around you in a new way—both the good and the bad. You're more in touch with what you're feeling and the feelings of others. The science behind this growth in empathy tells us that mothers develop a kind of sixth sense toward emotional perceptiveness as a way to perceive threats to our offspring and expand our ability to love and nurture another human.[13]

Adam Franssen says, "I think that's the brain rewiring. It is rewiring from, okay, I have a standard reaction to other individuals, or a standard amount of empathy, and that empathy is now increasing so that I can better protect my offspring when it gets here."[14]

Empathy helps us as mothers, as humans, and as employees and leaders. As moms, we're able to deeply connect to what other people are going through. We can feel when something is emotionally "off." We can also sense when *we're* off. And we figure out how to show up, how to execute, regardless of how we're feeling.

There's a term for this: emotional intelligence. *Psychology Today* defines emotional intelligence as "the ability to identify and manage one's own emotions, as well as the emotions of others."[15]

Managing the emotions of others is half the job description of a parent. It's what we do without even realizing it. We're used to navigating the stormy waters of toddlerhood, when the wrong color of spoon can create a fissure in the foundations of the earth. You want me to walk into a boardroom and manage the emotions of adults with fully developed frontal lobes? Piece of cake.

A working mom's ability to feel is one of the reasons half the country would rather work for her. Millennials in particular place a high value on work culture. Writing for *Forbes*, Caroline Castrillon says, "They want to work at organizations that champion values like compassion, collaboration, and the freedom to be yourself."[16]

I did an interview series for CARRY Media with working moms in Chicago, and I met a brilliant mom named Brittney. I asked Brittney what her superpower as a working mom is. Brittney said, "My superpower is…compassion. I grew up in a household where it was, you do great and that's just the expectation… Whereas now, with my boys, I'm reminding them, especially as Black men, that you can show emotion, and as long as you help us understand why, we can work through that. The same for my husband…I encourage him to do the same. It's okay to cry, or it's okay to laugh, or it's okay to be silly, or it's okay to be angry. But help me understand the why behind it and then we work through it that way."

If every company in America was headed by someone with the ability to relate, the ability to be self-aware and emotionally intelligent, and the ability to give their teams permission to feel their feelings, and then was given the help to process those feelings, how drastically would the mental health crisis in the workplace (which is at an all-time high in our country[17]) change?

Problem-Solving and Innovation Skills

If there's anything a mom knows how to do, it's troubleshooting.

I will legit pass out if I see blood. It activates some sort of psychological reaction in me that I can't explain. There's some psychology behind it, but it makes me too light-headed to read up on it. As a mother to two high-energy boys and an athletic daughter, blood has been a regular occurrence in our household. But no blood incident was bloodier than the time JJ busted open his scalp.

JJ thought he'd test out his flight skills by trying to run and dive over the couch. To his credit, he did clear it. What he didn't clear was the corner of the coffee table, which caught him right upside the head. He sat up and I saw two things: (1) exposed scalp and (2) squirting blood.

Nightmare.

My knees immediately gave way, and I felt dizzy. But I was the only grown-up in the house, and I knew I had to get him to urgent care immediately. So I troubleshot the situation, by delegating.

"Caroline!" I yelled. "Get a washcloth. Prop up your brother's head on a pillow."

I coached my elementary-aged daughter in first aid while I packed up a diaper bag, my toddler, keys, and insurance cards. We were out of the house in under five minutes. And I'm happy to report that I managed to pass out zero times in the process.

There's a saying usually attributed to Plato that "desperation is the mother of invention." That truth drives a lot of the accomplishments of women at home and at work. We're the end of the line. The goalie. The buck stops with us as the default. We know that, often, if we don't do it, don't fix it, don't address it, don't clean it—it won't get done. I'm convinced that moms are the masters of innovation and invention. Not because we're sitting around in a laboratory with our ideas and postulations, but because we're desperate!

In fact, over the years, women have invented some pretty cool gadgets. And every single one of them was born out of an acute need for a better way. You have to hear about some of these women[18]—it's fascinating what we're capable of.

- In 1893 Margaret Wilcox invented the car heater by creating a system to channel air over the engine and into the cab.
- In 1899 Letitia Greer invented the one-handed syringe. Before her innovation, medical professionals were required to use two hands to give injections.
- While translating some notes on the Analytical Engine for mathematics professor Charles Babbage, Ada Lovelace tripled the length of the original text with her own notes. She is credited with writing the very first computer algorithm in 1843.
- Mary Anderson got a patent for her windshield wiping device in 1903. When she tried to sell her idea to a manufacturer, she was turned down because they said windshield wipers held no practical value.
- In 1914, Florence Parpart dreamed up the electric refrigerator to replace the cumbersome iceboxes.
- And in the glorious year 1872, Josephine Cochran created a dishwasher that cleaned dishes using water pressure. Josephine, God love you.

A woman invented the circular saw. The first aquarium. The globe, the locomotive chimney, the life raft, the fire escape, the ironing board, the retractable dog leash, the coffee filter, the foot pedal trash can, central heating, the disposable diaper (no surprise there), bullet-proof fiber, the home security system, caller ID, space station batteries, naturally colored cotton, stem cell isolation, and the space rocket propulsion system.

One of my favorite female innovators is a woman named El Dorado Jones. First of all, what an incredible name. El Dorado Jones's nickname was Iron Woman. She invented the airplane muffler in 1917. But the coolest thing about El Dorado is that she owned her own metalworking factory in the early 1900s, where she only employed women over the age of forty. El Dorado, you are my people. You are the only Jones I'd like to keep up with!

If you're connected to the business world, you've probably heard a lot of chatter recently about the value of innovation in the workplace. As organizations are trying to become more competitive in a challenging market, women must have a seat at the table—at every table. Women, and especially working moms, not only bring a new perspective, but they come with a roll-up-your-sleeves, there's-gotta-be-a-solution mindset. And if there isn't an existing solution, we'll invent one.

• • • • •

One of the reasons moms are so valuable in the workplace is that we're short on excuses and long on fulfilling our commitments. We just get it done.

Another one of the moms I met during the CARRY Media interviews in Chicago is Lauren Jackson, a single mom and mental health therapist. When I asked Lauren what a typical day in her life looks like, she said, "Twenty-two hours of work and two hours of sleep." I about fell out of my chair. I asked her to repeat herself, and she did—and she was *smiling*. "That is what my day looks like," she said. "I work overnights in trauma. I do that so that I can be available to my daughter during the day."

Lauren represents the essence of what being a working mom is—we get it done. Why? Because of our why. We know what we're doing matters, because we've got little eyes following us, watching as we carry our work *and* carry our families.

A lot of moms work because they want to, but an increasing number of moms enter the workforce because they have to. We've already talked about how the rise in the cost of living combined with stagnant wages has demanded that most families become dual-income households. But the data tells us that the pressure on women is higher than ever before.

In my interview with Jennifer Glass, she referenced a study she took part in that revealed a staggering statistic: 70 percent of moms can be expected to be the breadwinner for their families at some point while their children are still minors.[19] This is true across all demographics.

And yet, the earnings of mothers fall behind fathers by as much as 30 percent.[20] The "mom tax," as it's called, is essentially a penalty women experience in the workplace. But when you assess the innate value of being a working mom—even objectively—the disparity in pay (and opportunity) just doesn't make sense.

This isn't just a problem for working moms—it's a problem for our country. If action isn't taken, debt will rise, poverty will increase, and families will suffer. But change is possible. Change is already happening every day. We see it through our work at CARRY. And there are so many organizations stepping up and getting it right. But we need *more*. Not just working moms—our country, culture, and our families need more.

Janet Van Huysse was the eightieth employee hired at Twitter. After working her way up the ranks, she was the only female executive at the company for many years. She was also the first person in the history of Twitter to take a maternity leave. Our friend Amy Henderson of TendLab interviewed Janet about parents in the workplace.

"The companies who will succeed in the twenty-first century," Janet said, "will be the ones who recognize that parents are an asset to an organization. The skills acquired by parenting are the same skills they need in their leader."[21]

Amy explains, "As automation continues to replace roles formerly held by people, many of the remaining positions will be those only humans can fill." This will require companies to seek out talent that can connect, perceive, emote, understand, and relate. If that's not the job description of a mother, I don't know what is.

> "The companies who will succeed in the twenty-first century," Janet said, "will be the ones who recognize that parents are an asset to an organization. The skills acquired by parenting are the same skills they need in their leader."

When I asked Jessica Kim, a Boston mom of three and CEO and co-founder of Iana Care, a network that provides support for caretakers, what she'd say if she could go back in time and give her "pre-mom" self-advice, here's what she said:

"Girlfriend, you're going to cry. You're going to be exhausted. There's going to be times when you want to give up. There are going to be times where you think, *Is this all worth it? Am I doing everything well? Am I being the mom that I want to be? Am I giving my work all that I want to give?* You're going to see that the world is unfair. You're going to see that systems aren't built for you. You may think that it's just completely impossible." But what I would also tell her is, "You just need to persevere, that we need you out there. That you're going to be part of that change, that if you break it down into phases and stages, that you will find a medium and it's not going to be perfect. There's nothing perfect, but we [have] to redefine what perfection is, and you've got to keep going and then build up the generation that's following you. Because if we don't, society is going to completely crumble and be a world that we don't even want our kids to live in."

Moms have scientific advantages as employees. We do a lot when given a little. Our multitasking skills defy space and time. Our brains and compassion grow with each child we give life to. We're not a liability. We're an asset. We've got to keep going, keep using our voices, and keep fighting. As working moms, we carry scientific superpowers in our homes and our offices. We carry a need that we uniquely fill. We carry innate value. We carry superpowers. And, if we're not already doing so, we need to carry each other.

HOW TO ASK FOR A RAISE[22]

- Ask for what you deserve. Men ask for raises four times more than women, and when they do, they ask for 30 percent more.

- Consider the best time to ask for a raise. Good times are when you've been doing exceptionally well, when you've worked in the same position for at least six months, or when you've taken on additional responsibilities.

- Toot your own horn. Have a minimum of three achievements written down and note any favorable reviews your manager has completed with you in recent years.

- Set a goal. Make sure you've looked at salary range comps. Choose a number that's high enough for your boss to counter with an acceptable offer.

- Be willing to compromise. There may be other possibilities on the table, such as flex schedule, vacation time, time off, stock options. Would you be willing to take any of these in lieu of a raise?

- Practice your pitch. Rehearse in front of a mirror or with friends or coworkers. Work out the kinks and hesitancies ahead of time.

CHAPTER SEVEN

CARRY EACH OTHER

Being a single mom in the entertainment industry, I always have to hustle to keep working. Stand-up comedy, speaking, hosting talk shows—all require me to travel—and Jeffrey is in school so he can't travel with me. I just hope one day he will look up and realize that I made a lot of sacrifices for him and that I did what I loved.

—Sherri Shepherd, actor and stand-up comic

The sweetest thing just happened to me at a Love's gas station in Blacksburg, South Carolina. We were driving back from Caroline's volleyball tournament, starving, and a little out of it. You know, the stage that's one step past hangry? Delirium?

A gas station attendant noticed Landon had wandered off as we were picking up snacks, and she mentioned it to me in a totally nonjudgmental way. Her name was Kirby. I thanked her and started to direct the troops back to the car so I could devour my processed sugars without losing a child.

As we were leaving, Kirby said, "Has anyone told you today you're a good mama? I don't have any kids, but you're a good mama, and you should know that today."

That stopped me in my tracks. I almost cried, that's how much it meant to me. I got to my car and wrote down the interaction, so I'd remember to share it with you. It illustrates the challenge I want to issue in this chapter so very well: If we want things to improve for working moms, women must choose to carry each other in this fight.

Kirby did two things: (1) She kept an eye out for my kid when I was unaware. She was her brother's keeper (or, in this case, her sister's keeper). (2) She gave me unsolicited encouragement in a moment when I might have been embarrassed or frustrated.

That made my day. If I had had more energy, I'd have wept.

How different would our country be if we all followed Kirby's lead, if we all took two simple steps to carry each other?

When I was transitioning from living in New York to where we are now in South Carolina, I was talking to a girlfriend about my decision to leave TV news and move to the South. I don't know what I was looking for at that moment, but it wasn't what I got. My friend was quiet for a moment, and then she said: "Paula, you've built an incredible name for yourself in news. You can't just disappear into the ether."

She didn't say, "I'm so glad you're going to spend more time with your family. You can do this."

She said, "You can't disappear into the ether."

The ether being less visibility professionally and more visibility personally.

Her words lingered. In fact, I've had them written in my notes for writing this book from the moment I dreamed about writing it. I know her concern was genuine, but it only served to reinforce my insecurities about what was ahead for me. Those words didn't cheer for me or cheer for my family. They were indicting.

I could talk for hours on the ways I've been railed at by other women—other mothers—very publicly for the way I choose to raise my children. There was the miscarriage incident with Caroline, but that wasn't an isolated event. I'm positive you have a multitude of stories, too.

Here's what I know: I am not the only mother who has been ridiculed by other mothers. You've experienced it too, unless you live in some secret city of peace and serenity—in which case, I'll be right over, bottle of tequila in hand.

MOMMY WARS

If you walk the streets of New York City on a weekday morning, you'll spot two types of women rushing by at an equally frenzied pace: women carrying laptop bags and women pushing strollers. These women don't cross party lines. The bag holders do not make eye contact with the stroller pushers and vice versa. It's as if they're from different camps. Like they're playing for different teams.

But shouldn't we all value families? That's one jersey we should all wear proudly. Remember what Amy Henderson from TendLab said? The state and health of the American family is the barometer for economic and political stability in our country.[1]

As an executive at the *Washington Post*, mama-to-three Leslie Morgan Steiner is familiar with the mommy wars, which is the apt title to the book she wrote on how a mother's decision to either work or stay home has become a divisive and almost hostile topic in our country.[2] Leslie invited twenty-six outspoken moms to submit essays about their families and how their choice to stay home or to work has affected their lives.

In her book, Leslie recounts an experience at a friend's birthday party where she was explaining the idea behind the project to a few other moms. When a stay-at-home mom joined the conversation, Leslie's friend, a question-probing journalist like me, asked her what she thought about moms who work.

Leslie writes about her response:

Without breathing, the stay-at-home mom answered, "Oh, I feel *so* sorry for them."…This woman felt sorry for me? For all the moms…who work to support their families, to show their kids women can work, who work to change the world, who work to keep their sanity?

My reporter friend was watching me closely. "She doesn't feel sorry for *me* or *you*…She feels sorry *in theory* for women who work. It's why she doesn't work. Because she imagines that if you work, you don't have time for your children, your husband, life. She doesn't know what it's really like to work. Just like you and I don't know what it's really like to stay home full-time. That's why you're writing this book—so we can end this catfight."[3]

If you look at the titles of the essays in Leslie's book, you'll see just how right her friend is. Here are just a few:

"The Mother Load"
"Baby Battle"

"Guilty"

"Mother Superior"

"Good Enough"

"I Hate Everybody"

"I Do Know How She Does It"

"I Never Dreamed I'd Have So Many Children"

"Russian Dolls"

"Unprotected"

"Julia"

"My Baby's Feet Are Size 13"

You know what I noticed about the majority of the essay titles? You can't tell which ones come from stay-at-home moms and which ones come from moms in the workforce. That suggests to me what I've always felt to be true: We're not very different from one another—not nearly as different as we act like we are.

By the way, can we please, for the love of all that's holy, stop referring to stay-at-home moms as such? Is there not another title, one that's even a tad more accurate and less demeaning, that we could come up with? I've done some sleuthing on the origin of the term, later in this chapter, which I cannot wait to share with you.

But back to the mommy wars.

At the crux of the mommy wars is a misunderstanding of another person's choice. But isn't that at the crux of almost every conflict? Do I really need to examine why any mother chooses anything for their families? Is it any of my business? In my experience with the mommy wars, we don't judge each other for hard-hitting parenting fails. We judge each other for

> At the crux of the mommy wars is a misunderstanding of another person's choice.

things like how short a middle schooler's dress was at the Valentine's Day dance.

> *"Can you believe she let her daughter wear that?"*
> *"He's still taking a pacifier? My son was weaned at six months."*
> *"She's going to be breastfeeding her daughter when she goes to college."*
> *"She never volunteers for carpool. She's always working."*
> *"I heard they're struggling financially, but she refuses to go to work. She feels 'called' to stay home."*

Ladies! We still earn almost 30 percent less than fathers for the same work. I say we start whispering about *that*—or shouting about that—not about what brand bottle our neighbor down the street uses for their baby. We need to give ourselves more credit. We're so much better than petty—we're brilliant, multitasking superheroes. Let's carry that anthem!

MOM GUILT CENTRAL

Leslie Steiner writes, "I don't understand moms who find happiness staying home all the time, without work and their own incomes (however large or small). I can't fathom why some working moms stay stuck in too-demanding jobs or careers that they openly resent because of the quality (and quantity) time they miss with their kids. But what I know for certain…is that the two groups misunderstand and envy each other in the corrosive, fake-smiling way we women have perfected over the eons."[4]

The other factor in our lack of mutual support is that green-eyed devil: envy. I think this is part of human nature, but it's also deeply connected to the pressure we feel as mothers. We question our own choices and wonder if maybe we've made the wrong ones. We look at another mother's life, and maybe it sparks a bit of envy. It leads us to fantasize about how our lives might be different.

> *If I didn't have to work...*
> *If childcare were more affordable...*
> *If my husband would help more...*
> *If I didn't miss my baby so much...*
> *If I weren't breastfeeding...*
> *If things weren't so expensive...*

We fantasize about life on the other side, and we feel we're coming up short. We feel that because of our decision, we're missing out on something. The infighting comes from a defensiveness—a defensiveness born of just wanting to do what's best combined with our very limited options. When we feel insecure, we poke holes in the lives of others, because in some way, we wonder if they're measuring up and we're not.

In my interviews for CARRY Media, I met a working mom named Diana from Charlotte, North Carolina. I asked her to name the source of her mom guilt and burnout. She said, "I think in certain circles, maybe even some circles that I'm a part of, it can feel like I'm the only one who's working or the only one who has to say, 'I can't meet you at the park today at one o'clock because I've got this call.' Being a working mom is difficult. Sometimes isolating. It's feeling like you're the only one who's in this place, and who's walking in the tension of wanting to be fully present in both places, but being one single human being."

Take my friend Melanie, the teacher who decided to stay home after fifteen years on the job. She is racked with guilt. She feels guilt about working, guilt about staying home, and guilt that she still wants to work outside the home in some capacity. CARRY's 2022 research found that 80 percent of the moms we surveyed are carrying some level of mom guilt.

My friend and NBC's *Today* host Savannah Guthrie told me, "I definitely feel torn anytime I'm away from my kids for many reasons. It's like mom guilt central. I can't believe how much that mom guilt thing is real…and when I first brought my daughter home, I felt guilty if she was in the next room. What makes you a good mom? I mean, is it the time that you spend, the love that you give, how much you are willing to pour into your kids? It's a constant inner battle."

Or take tennis goddess Serena Williams. She shared with *Insider* about her life as a working mom and professional athlete. Here's what she said: "I'm really bad at self-care…I was just telling my chief of staff that I need to get a pedicure because it's been two years since I sat in a chair and had one. Maybe I could do that while I'm multitasking and taking calls."[5]

This best-selling author and mom to preschooler Olympia confessed that while she can handle the woes of a busy schedule and motherhood, it's not always so black and white. She shared, "Mom guilt is real. I always feel so guilty when I'm doing something on my own."

Said every mom, ever—even ones with a chief of staff.

"JUST" A MOM

During my time on *The View*, I worked with co-host Candace Cameron Bure, maybe better known as D.J. Tanner from ABC's *Full House* and *Fuller House*. After breaking into show business at a young age, Candace married hockey star Valeri Bure in 1996 at age twenty, and shortly after had her first of three adorable kiddos.

For many of the years that followed, Candace chose to be a stay-at-home mom. On an episode of *The Motherly Podcast*, Candace talks about that experience: "It was so hard. I felt worthless. I felt like I had been gifted all of these things in life, whatever that is, whatever skills God gave me. And I thought, 'I'm not using them.'"[6]

Candace would often be recognized in public. When she was out shopping for groceries, strangers would stop and ask, "What are you up to these days?"

Though she dreaded their inevitable response, Candace would force a smile and say, "I'm a mom now." The result? "And it was like, they were always disappointed and which in turn made me feel even more like, oh my gosh, being a mom is…I'm 'just' a mom. Like this is not valued by society."

Do you hear what I hear? (Pause while I refrain from breaking out into this song.) No matter what you choose as a mother—to work outside the home or to "stay at home"—it's all hard. It's all challenging. It's all a juggling act. And you feel like you're disappointing someone no matter what. Why is that? Just who are we disappointing? Are our kids hurting? Is our partner hurting?

> No matter what you choose as a mother—to work outside the home or to "stay at home"—it's all hard. It's all challenging. It's all a juggling act.

Probably not. What we're feeling is this very American pressure to be something other than who we are. We (myself included) allow a nameless, faceless society to convince us that we just don't measure up.

Stay-at-home moms, we need you in this fight too. Working moms, we need each other. How can we stand in the gap for each other? We're going to get to that.

Before we move on toward a more practical look at carrying one another, let's pause to talk about the common titles given to us by modern culture:

- Stay-at-home mom
- Working mom

These feel a bit antiquated, right? Stay-at-home moms don't necessarily "stay at home." They go to the grocery store. They do Mommy-and-me music hours. They do carpool runs. They take the forgotten lunchbox to school. They play mystery reader for a class of second graders. They volunteer. They run by the bank and manage the finances. They pick up the dry cleaning. They may not be at the office every day, but the stay-at-home moms I know do not "stay" at home.

Let's take on the term *working mom*. First—and you've heard this said before—all moms work. If your kid is alive and fed, you've been working hard—extra hard in a house of picky eaters like mine. To say "Are you a working mom? Or do you stay home?" to a stay-at-home mom feels like a slight. The implied modifier there is "Are you *just* a stay-at-home mom?"

When someone says "working mom," the connotation is that you're less present as a mom. You're not taking photos in coordinating outfits and then posting #SAHM #SAHMLife #BestJobOnThePlanet selfies. (We're careful to assert the superiority of our parenting decisions, regardless of which side of the mommy wars we are on.)

In the same way, the *working mom* title reduces our roles as mothers as secondary to our work. If a stay-at-home mom is labeled for what she doesn't do (paid work), the same is true for a working mom. If you're a working mom, you're not really a "mom's mom." How often do we say, "Oh, she's leaving her career to raise her children." Isn't that implying that working moms are not raising theirs?

Even in our language, we're systemically pitted against one another.

Why does society want us to be just one thing? This hits at our identity crisis, because we don't neatly fit into one category. And I believe it contributes to our exhaustion and burnout and compulsion to carry it all, because in our search for identity, we're trying to be all things to all people, and that's just not possible.

> Why does society want us to be just one thing? This hits at our identity crisis, because we don't neatly fit into one category.

To be reduced to how we earn our money or how we choose to do family massively oversimplifies our significance and value.

From the day I found out I was pregnant with Caroline, I became a mom.

When I went back to work, I wasn't less of a mom.

When I moved to South Carolina and spent most days at home, I was still working.

I was working to establish my family in a new home, in a new state. And I was working my side hustle, which has now become way more than on the side.

I know tons of moms who don't fit into a checkable box. Moms who are at home but have a thriving nonprofit that they don't earn an income from. Moms who are at home, but work "off" hours ranging from full-time to part-time. I also know moms who are considered to be working moms by today's terms, but work from home with or without paid help.

So…what am I? A mom who stays at home and does paid work at increasingly growing intervals?

I recently overheard a conversation by a group of women where one said, "What does she do? Does she work or stay home?"

"Well, she does work," her friend explained, "but she's a teacher, so she's home when the kids are home."

It feels like we're all at a loss when it comes to describing our roles and how we function in our families. Is it by the amount of time our kids spend without us? Is it based on how many hours we're in an office outside of our houses?

SLAY-AT-HOME MOM

Katy Steinmetz did a story for *Time* back in 2014 that traces the history of the term "stay-at-home" mom, and believe it or not, it's relatively new.[7]

According to the article, the term *stay-at-home* originated in the 1800s, but it had nothing to do with mothers rearing children. "A talking pretty young woman like Miss Crawford," Jane Austen wrote in *Mansfield Park*, "is always pleasant society to an indolent, stay-at-home man."

Slate contributor Jessica Grose comes to the same conclusion in her article "Why Do We Call Them 'Stay-at-Home Moms'? There Must Be a Better Term."[8] She writes, "According to the etymology expert and University of Minnesota professor Anatoly Liberman, the term 'stay at home,' without the mom or dad tacked on, is very old. (Liberman recalls seeing the term in Dickens.) 'Stay at homes' were people who didn't travel."

According to Steinmetz's article, *housewife* is a term that's been around since the 1200s and was the general way to describe a mom who does not do paid work outside the home up until the mid-1900s. And we're back in the "Golden Age" again, aren't we? The 1950s gifted America not only its unsustainable nuclear-family model but also the term *homemaker*.

Steinmetz writes, "Homemaker, sociolinguist Ben Zimmer says, was seen as more respectful…The term also sounds less gendered, Zimmer says: 'A man, in theory, should be equally good at making the home.'"[9] Tell *that* to the 1950s housewife, Ben.

The *mom* addition to the phrase *stay-at-home* rose in popularity during the 1980s and became a part of the everyday vernacular by the 1990s, when women returned to the workforce in droves. The *New York Times* didn't use the phrase until 1992, and even then it was in quotes.[10]

In their research for their book *Your Turn: Careers, Kids, and Comebacks—A Working Mother's Guide*, Jennifer Gefsky and Stacey Delo came to the same conclusion I have: We need better terminology than *stay-at-home mom* to describe the dynamic of moms who either aren't paid for their work outside the home or are independently contracted to do work (non-salaried working moms).

"We've heard of sabbatical," they write in an article for the She Knows website, "independent contractor, choosing not to work outside of the home, former [fill in the blank] moonlighting as a mom. When we recently asked for new ideas, we heard 'Head of People Operations,' 'Mother Warrior,' 'Slay at Home Mom/Dad,' 'Family Coordinator,' 'Co-creator.' The list is long! A LinkedIn search yields even more suggestions, job titles and descriptions like 'Family leave.' 'Domestic engineer.' 'Pregnancy pause.' 'CEO of Jones Inc.' SAHM. And, simply, mom."[11]

I'd take any of these titles. Changing our language would be a good start. But ultimately I'd like the role of stay-at-home mom to be given more credit. That's the win, for society to acknowledge that we're not pausing our professional expertise when we pause salaried work.

These changes start with us—with moms—working for a salary or otherwise.

CARRYING EACH OTHER

Over the last three decades, it seems the lines between moms who work outside the home and stay-at-home moms have become more like minefields. I love the positive power of social media, but it would be naïve not to draw parallels between its emergence and the increase in awareness of what other moms are (and are not) doing and our impulse to comment on both.

A national poll of nearly five hundred moms conducted in 2017 by Michigan Medicine's C.S. Mott Children's Hospital found that the majority of them have felt mom-shamed.[12] I'm no sociologist, but I imagine that number has skyrocketed in response to the COVID-19 pandemic, when parents were asked to make impossible choices with ever-changing data and zero context to inform decisions.

Would we ever see a dad's social media post about spending time with his kids, screenshot it to a friend, and say, "What is he *thinking*? What kind of parent is *he*?"

My guess is no.

If we want to understand why women are fair game for criticism in corporate America, maybe we should start by asking why they're fair game in our own lives and circles.

Women in C-level executive positions have to reach down and help the next woman up the ladder. Heck—if you're a woman with a seat at *any* table, create a place setting beside you for another woman to sit down. You may have to nudge or encourage the hosts to get her there, but get her that invite.

> If we want to understand why women are fair game for criticism in corporate America, maybe we should start by asking why they're fair game in our own lives and circles.

We've got to stop tearing each other down. I'm not sure women will ever stop picking each other apart, but I can sure try to mitigate senseless gossip as much as possible. It's a waste of valuable energy, friends. And it's doing us no favors. When we criticize the way another mom parents, we're tossing gasoline-soaked logs onto the fire that's devouring our potential.

What does carrying each other look like in everyday life? It looks like…

- Accepting that the way we parent isn't the only "best" way.
- Refusing to give in to a superior or passive-aggressive attitude toward moms who mom a different way than we do.

- Reaching down the ladder and bringing up the woman behind us.
- Encouraging one another publicly and being each other's biggest cheerleaders and champions.
- Apologizing for the times we haven't carried each other but instead let each other down.
- Admitting you need help sometimes.

We heard from founder and CEO Jessica Kim earlier. When I asked her how she balanced being a mom of three and the leader of a family caregiving organization, she admitted to not being good at asking for help early on and trying to carry it all.

"I'm a recovering 'independent' mom," Jessica said, "who rarely asked for help despite desperately needing it. I've burned myself out and realized how truly lonely it is to be the one doing it all. I now seek a tribe. I'm vulnerable enough to share when I'm struggling and I allow people to help."

In *Tending*, Amy Henderson interviewed evolutionary anthropologist Sarah Hrdy and learned "several critical things" about how moms have evolved over history. "First, a woman's ability to develop and maintain her 'maternal instinct' is highly dependent on the level of support she receives."[13] Amy learned that if a woman doesn't have people surrounding her to help carry the load, she risks the inability to "bond with and care for her child."

WE NEED HELP. IT'S NOT WEAKNESS, IT'S NOT FAILURE—IT'S HUMANITY.

Amy Henderson writes of her own experience as a mother: "Up until that moment, I hadn't wanted to admit, even to myself, how much I was struggling. Even though I knew intellectually that other moms must also be having a hard time, I imagined that my situation was worse—either because of me and my unique shortcomings, or because of the bad decisions I'd made."

Sound familiar? I can relate. I spent *years* questioning my approach to motherhood—especially when I was working in broadcast television. I would think, *Why does everyone else have it together but me? Is it my job? Am I not meant to be a mom? Am I not meant to work outside the home?* Even with live-in childcare, I didn't feel as if I was getting the job done well *anywhere*.

Like me, Amy, says she conceded to herself that she was "incapable of handling it all," but for a while, her shame prevented her from getting the help she knew she needed.[14]

Amy's story and my story are the reason I wrote this book. I heard these same sentiments echoed in the lives and experiences of moms I met everywhere. But that narrative can change.

I was recently exchanging horror stories from parenting with a friend who has always been a stay-at-home mom. I was telling her how my kid had seen me wearing a thong (which is not the norm for me) and said, "Mom, why is your butt eating your underwear?"

Here's what I know about us. We've *all* got a story like that. My mom sure does. I've given her plenty of fodder. Take, for instance, the time she caught me as a child drinking that "water bottle" I found under her sink. Which turned out was her douche bottle. I think she may have suffered a mild heart attack before she yanked it from my hands. We're all moms. At the end of the day, shouldn't that bond be stronger than our impulse to criticize?

#MOMFAIL

At the time I was writing this book, I posted an "all-call" to my Instagram stories asking for moms to share some of their most embarrassing moments in momming. I wish I could share all of them here. They're hilarious. I think if we all knew just how hard others were trying, and just how desperately many of us want to measure up but feel like we don't, we'd be a whole lot kinder to one another.

Here's a few of those #MomFail moments:

1. My friend Emma shared about an experience where she was trying to carry it all and ended up quite...*exposed*. She and her hubby were planning their first time away in years. They were going on an eight-day exotic trip. Emma was trying to be a wife, trying to be a mom, trying to be a business owner. There wasn't a lot of time to take care of her own body. Her daughter is in fourth grade. She picked her up from school before leaving for the trip, trying to spend one-on-one time with her while out running errands. Emma told her daughter she needed to go to a place to get waxed. When her fourth grader asked what waxing was, Emma explained waxing is for eyebrows and "other" unwanted body hair.

   She asked her daughter to wait in the reception area with her book (she's an avid reader). Emma told her daughter, "I'll be right back," went into the waxing room, and told the waxologist, "I'm going away with my husband for eight days—it's all coming off."

   If you aren't familiar with the tedious task of Brazilian waxes: You have to grow out all the "other" unwanted hair prior to getting waxed in order for it to be effective. Right in the middle of the wax job, the door to the room opened with Emma on the table. "Mommy, what are you doing in here?" her daughter yelled.

"I'm getting a wax. Could you *please* shut the door?"

The door was *wide open* with Emma in a compromising waxing position, so anyone walking by could see.

Emma is a total trooper, because she finished the job, paid, and got her kid back into the car without wilting like a flower in the sun. Afterward, she had to explain everything to her daughter—*everything*.

"But," Emma said, "I still looked great on the trip."

2. A follower named Sylvia responded to my all-call with this story: "My #MomFail story is that whenever I accidentally hurt myself, like stub my toe or burn my hand on the stove, I say a certain curse word. But [the curse word I say] is in German (the country I was born in). Now my four-year-old knows and says this German cuss word because he thinks it's funny but has no idea what it means! (For context: My dad is an American Army officer and my mom is German, so that makes me an Army brat…The wurst)."

3. Another follower named Chrissy wrote: "Funny epic mom fail…My son who was two at the time literally ate my daughter's art project. Had no clue, but for like two days he wouldn't eat or take the bottle. I was stumped, and thought he was sick. Nope. The babysitter found a googly eye stuck to the roof of his mouth. Obviously, the art project was tasty, but he really didn't like the googly eye. Luckily, he didn't choke. It's funny now, not so much then."

4. My friend Diana Carter, a mom of two who owns Carter

House Copy, said: "I feel embarrassed to admit mom fails only three years into mumming, but this summer, I accidentally locked our son in our minivan in the heat of summer. I had to call 911 and a firetruck came to break him out of our car. I was in a rush and left my keys on the front seat. At the very least, he LOVED the firetruck. He wasn't bothered one bit, but I cried, haha." I know Diana personally, and she's the *last* mom I'd expect to have a #MomFail. This is a lady who once ran a 5K in under eighteen minutes. She's incredibly impressive. Her story reminded me that you will be both impressive *and* imperfect as a mother.

5. A follower named Stacy wrote in as well: "One of my many #MomFails. My youngest son was probably 11ish. He was telling me that his older brother got all of the attention. He felt like he was not noticed and left out. I was trying to console him and I said, 'Oh, Snickers. You know that is not true.' I called him by the dog's name. I will never forget the look on his face as he said, 'Point made.'"

I don't have all the answers, but I do know this: When we stand *for* something, we're so much more powerful than when we stand *against* something. Division doesn't create change. Join together with your sisters (and, yes, your brothers) in parenthood. Let's refuse to feed misogyny by using our big, beautiful brains and our loud, vibrant voices to encourage and lift one another up. When we carry each other, there's absolutely nothing that can hold us down.

CHAPTER EIGHT

CARRY ON, MY WAYWARD SON

I really believe the only way that we can heal is if we can share our stories so that other people can find their own. And a lot of us men are not comfortable talking about these things.

—Justin Baldoni, actor, filmmaker, and author

I used to think that giving my kids 100 percent of my attention was the best thing I could do for them. I now believe that it is best for them to see themselves not as the thing our family revolves around, but as part of a family that serves each other. It's important for them to see me with my own goals, priorities, interests, etc., apart from them. I make sure they know how important they are to us, but also that they aren't the center of our universe.

—Cynthia, high school English teacher and mom of two

I've caught myself on several occasions telling my boys to "man up" or to "be a man" about it. As I began to think about this chapter, I asked our oldest son, JJ, how he felt when I told him to "be a man."

He said, "It bothers me sometimes."

I pressed a little more. "When you hear people in our culture talk about what it means to be a man, what does that mean to you?"

"To be respectful and kind. To stand up for other people."

"And when I tell you, 'JJ, be a man about it.' What does *that* mean?"

"To grow up and not be, like, scared or something. I don't know."

I love that kid. He's such a twelve-year-old. He's perfect.

Being a man has different connotations in our culture. When someone says to "man up," it's a way of saying to be a "real" man. My husband said this about the term: "When I think about what a 'real' man is in America, I picture a gritty cowboy doing whatever he wants. He's tough. When someone says, 'man up,' they're asking you to stop being soft."

When it comes to being a good man, however, John says the messages are different. "Being a good man means to be a good father, a good husband, a good employee or employer. It means treating others well."

John's and JJ's answers hit at the heart of the dual messages sent to our young men as they are developing: A good man is sensitive and caring, but a real man is strong and fearless. Is it possible to be both of these things at once? Is it feasible to be both a "good" and "real" man?

As the director of the Center for the Study of Men and Masculinities at Stony Brook University, Michael Kimmel has dedicated his career to understanding what it means to be a man in America today. In his class on the study of masculinities, he asks students to answer the following two questions:

1. What does it mean to be a "good" man?
2. What does it mean to be a "real" man?

For a "good" man, the typical responses are *honest, caring, a good husband and father, hardworking, dependable, sensitive,* and *selfless.*

For a "real" man, the responses are not the same. Words like *strong, independent, intimidating, confident, attractive,* and *detached* are used.

I did another all-call on my social media for men or spouses of followers to answer those two questions. Here's what some followers said.

One message came in from a pastor. "I hear from society that a 'good man' works hard to provide for his family, look after his wife and kids, and do whatever needs to be done to make 'it' happen," he said. "The message I get about what a 'real man' is to 'suck it up' and deal with it, feelings are not your friends, just keep moving forward, and nobody cares, so keep it to yourself. Most of the time I hear that a good man is kind but soft, whereas a real man is tough and rugged—not to be messed with. As a kid it felt like you couldn't be both. You either choose the kind, soft route, or the tough, manly shut-your-mouth-and-get-it-done way of life."

Another response came in from a therapist who works with military veterans. "I hear some messages that are helpful, and some that aren't. In my field it's been cool to see one's mental health being uncoupled from masculinity. Spending time with hypermasculine combat veterans who are also able to do things we perceive as feminine—be the primary childcare provider, talk about feelings, cry—has been encouraging. I think a lot of men feel challenged trying to navigate new ways in which it's OK to be more 'feminine,' while also maintaining old ways of masculinity."

What he said next really fascinated me, and it helped me understand the tension for a lot of men. "More flexibility with gender roles has been accompanied by increased confusion and ambivalence for me and a lot of other men I talk to. We have more decisions to make, more choices to struggle with. My dad's generation (in my community) didn't tend to question the more rigid gender roles of the time, but I'm learning to take on traditionally feminine roles and ways of being/thinking in a way that wasn't really modeled for me. And, of course, achievement continues to be highly tied to the concept of masculinity. Being able to demonstrate success with respect to finances, kids, marriage always seems to have a lot of social currency attached to it."

Interesting takes, right? Asking the meaning of the terms *good man* and a *real man* might be an eye-opening exercise you can conduct with the men in your life, too.

Emotionally speaking, we've asked men to carry it all—to embody two extremes, sensitive and stoic, depending on what *we* need from men at any given moment.

"I think American men are confused about what it means to be a man,"[1] Michael Kimmel says. The consequences of which are very serious.

"This stuff is all around us," he explained to *New York Times* journalist Jessica Bennett. "We have a mass shooter in the U.S.

every few weeks. And every time it happens, we talk about guns. We talk about mental health. But we don't talk about how all of these mass shooters are male…We need to understand how masculinity affected their experience."[2]

Daphne C. Watkins, the president of American Men's Studies Association (and the first woman to fill the role), explains that "We're looking at [the study of masculinity] as a science…Many men still define masculinity as someone who can provide for his family, who can wrestle a tiger and protect…What I would love to see is for us to broaden those definitions."[3]

Broadening those definitions means we have to first recognize the toxic expectations words like *masculinity* and *patriarchy* carry with them.

APOLOGIZING FOR THAT
Y CHROMOSOME

American actor and filmmaker Justin Baldoni has a lot of great things to say about masculinity. He gave the vulnerable TED Talk "Why I'm Done Trying to Be 'Man Enough,'" and this led to him writing the book *Man Enough: Undefining My Masculinity*. His desire was to take himself and other men out of the constricting box of masculinity.

"I didn't realize how much I was suffering," he said on *The Kelly Clarkson Show*. "So many men I know are suffering but we can't ask for help. We can't talk about it, because if we talk about it we're challenging the system that keeps us in the box."[4]

In a world where so many women are justifiably hurt and angry, Baldoni says that men often don't believe they have a voice.

"I really believe the only way that we can heal is if we can share our stories so that other people can find their own. And a lot of us men are not comfortable talking about these things."

I was recently reminded of what these toxic expectations could look like. While sitting in the stands of one of Caroline's volleyball tournaments recently, I struck up a conversation with the dad sitting beside me. If you're ever caught in close quarters with me for an extended amount of time, let me apologize in advance. I'm a journalist at a molecular level. Questions will be asked. Answers will be procured. I'm sorry. This is who I am.

We talked about our kids, about the volleyball season, about the town we were both in for the tournament. Eventually, he said, "You know, you look familiar."

I get this occasionally. But more often than not, people think I'm related to Anna Faris. (I'm not, by the way—our last names are just spelled the same).

I told him I'm a journalist, and I named a few of the shows I used to be on. My former life.

"That's it!" he said. "I used to watch you on the early morning show. So what are you up to now?"

CARRY Media had just been launched. And like the mother of a newborn, I doted proudly on my baby business, rambling about the work we're doing to champion the mama on her workplace journey. It took a couple of minutes, but I realized my volleyball buddy had gotten quiet. I finished talking, and he shifted uncomfortably. His eyes darted toward the exit sign behind the courts. He was planning his escape.

"That's good," he mumbled, nodding, starting at the double doors longingly. "That's great. You know...I *am* sorry."

"You're sorry?" I asked. "What are you sorry for?"

"Well." He laughed nervously. "I guess I'm sorry for being a man."

On the way home that night, I thought about his words. *Is that how all men feel? That they're sorry for being born male?* And more than that, *If that is how all men feel, then we've got more problems than a pay gap.*

Our problem—or one of the more pressing ones—is that there hasn't been enough clarity on what a man's role is in helping to eliminate gender disparities and lessen the load of moms carrying it all. And to be honest, we've thrown a lot of mixed messages at men—including that they're horrible human beings and the world would be better off without them. No wonder guys might be a tad hesitant to join us on the battle lines.

"Men Aren't the Enemy." That's the first chapter of author and journalist Joanne Lipman's book *That's What She Said: What Men Need to Know (and What Women Need to Tell Them) about Working Together*. I wish I could cite every word in that chapter here.

She starts off with a story similar to mine. She was on a plane and told the man beside her that she was going to speak at a women's conference. Like my volleyball buddy, he immediately apologized for being a man. (Lots of men apologizing for that Y chromosome these days.)

The next morning she spoke to several hundred women about issues women deal with at work. Issues like being ignored in meetings and being underestimated by male colleagues and seeing men receiving credit for their ideas. As the women in the hotel ballroom nodded their heads in agreement with her, Lipman paused midsentence.

"We already know all of this," she said. "We need men in this room to hear the message instead."[5]

> Understanding that many men enter the conversation on gender equality already feeling inadequate is the first step in carrying our invitation to engage.

One way men can hear this message is to invite them to enter into the conversation. Understanding that many men enter the conversation on gender equality already feeling inadequate is the first step in carrying our invitation to engage.

PUTTING DREAMS ON HOLD

We need to break down the notion that men are the enemy. Women can be critical of men for not being more engaged, but the truth is, they are burned out, too. Men are oppressed by expectations as well.

One particular expectation comes around the values our society assigns to men. As I mentioned earlier in this book, sociology professor Jennifer Glass explores the tragedy of the cultural message that a man's sole or primary value is to provide materially for his children as opposed to spending time with them, getting to know them, and building a strong relationship with them.

"We've made men feel like their only value is as a breadwinner," she told me. "We've made women feel like their only value is as a caregiver."

Glass explains that beginning with the rise in the middle class during the nineteenth century and into the first half of the twentieth century, during America's postwar prosperity, fathers were kicked out of the family while mothers were booted out of the workforce.

"The promise was if women were kicked out of labor and men kicked out of the home, you had someone raising kids and self-sufficiency. But it backfired because the bonds of obligation were weak. It was the family that paid the price at the end of the day."

I can only imagine what our family would have looked like if John had believed the lie that his only value was to be the breadwinner. He definitely wouldn't have stepped back from his own career and dreams to allow me to pursue mine.

John grew up in Indiana, and that meant the two most important things were high school basketball and Indiana University basketball. He loved both, so he played basketball and aspired to win the state championship. He became the third leading scorer in Indiana high school history when he graduated from high school back in 1995.

John played basketball at Cedarville University, the Division II school where we met. He had to really contemplate what he was going to do after he graduated from college. Going overseas and playing professionally didn't seem ideal, especially since we had just started dating. I never asked him to, but he chose me over playing basketball in another country. John was realistic and knew there was an expiration date on playing the game. That's why he chose coaching, because he could stay in the game and continue to be competitive.

As I shared earlier in this book, after getting married, John and I lived in Ohio, and he coached basketball. When I had a job opportunity in Chicago, John never hesitated. He pivoted and put his coaching dreams on hold for a new opportunity in a big city. He said that what I was doing was rare, and that only 1 percent of the population had an opportunity like this.

I think John also said something along the lines of "I don't think your face is always going to look like that. I can get back into coaching when I'm a dirty dog and seventy years old." That was John's way of acknowledging one of the ridiculous double standards between men and women.

Since his father had been in real estate, he had always wanted to own and invest in properties. So he got into residential real estate with a great company and found success there. We easily could have stayed in Chicago long-term; we had no reason to leave. But then a bigger opportunity opened up for me in New York.

Once again, John never hesitated. He viewed these open doors as new opportunities and challenges that God was giving us, so we were both excited to go through them. But if he had subscribed to some of the toxic expectations of a man's place and position as a provider, we might never have moved to either Chicago or New York.

There have been many times when John has been called Mr. Faris, and he's never corrected anyone. He's even worn a name tag that said "John Faris." It doesn't bother him. He realizes that I'm known by my maiden name. He also knows who he is and is confident in his identity.

That doesn't mean he doesn't have self-respect or pride.

When I was the primary breadwinner (we'll deconstruct this term, too) in our home for fifteen years, I used a certain phrase in our family: "Not only do I bring home the bacon, I have to fry it, too."

John hates that saying. First off, he knows it's not true, but he also thinks it's condescending in many ways. The truth is that marriage is a partnership. But what would it look like to break out of our assigned gender roles and carry one another in partnership?

ON MISSION

Ruth Chou Simons and Troy Simons are the embodiment of what a partnership looks like in a marriage. I've already spoken about Ruth earlier in this book. After I met Ruth at a women's retreat and learned that she and Troy have six boys, my first thought was, *My gosh, she's probably doing laundry all...the...time.*" So when I learned she doesn't cook, clean, or do the laundry in her house, my mind was blown. I knew I needed to have Ruth and Troy on my podcast.

For two decades, Troy was the founder and headmaster of a classical school. He was in charge of a staff and hundreds of students while Ruth was at home raising their six boys. In the wee hours of the night, Ruth would paint and blog as an outlet and for her personal growth.

Early on, Ruth and Troy thought of themselves as partners. She realized that she wasn't just a stay-at-home mom and he wasn't just the provider.

"He and I are doing the work together," Ruth said. "It doesn't matter if we're working for somebody else or we're working for ourselves. We know what we're about. We are on mission to make our lives count together."

Six years ago, Troy and Ruth saw their roles reversed as the blog Ruth created in 2007 became a multifaceted company called GraceLaced. Now, Troy is what the world would call a stay-at-home dad, but Ruth never refers to him as that. She's the breadwinner, but she doesn't refer to herself as that.

> "We are on mission to make our lives count together."

Ruth and Troy are "on mission" together as partners. They

could legit teach a master class on it. They don't compete. They work as a team. And they converse with their kids about the work they're doing in whatever season they're in.

"I definitely grew up where there was this bifurcation between men's work and women's work," Troy said. "There is a load that comes with being a couple and then most certainly being parents that is shared."

Ruth and Troy are challenging the idea that a dad should go to a job and work his butt off for eighteen hours while the mom manages things at home. And they're inviting their six sons into this conversation of how boys should become men and what that looks like.

A HUMAN CAUSE

The statistics for working moms are not encouraging. They do not reflect a country that values mothers or even a country that really values families. Our frustration is righteous and our discomfort has been long-suffering. Yet too often we forget to carry an invitation for men to engage in the conversation.

Too often our anger can turn into shaming.

I recently did one of those fasting diets. I wasn't supposed to eat after six p.m. and couldn't break my fast until eleven a.m. the next day.

I did not fare well.

I found myself in front of the fridge at ten p.m. most nights, eating slices of salami right out of the deli bag and an entire bag of baked puffs (they're baked—how bad can they be?). Then I'd go to bed, feeling guilty and defeated, promising I wouldn't repeat my binge the next night.

But I did.

For the entire time I participated in this intermittent fasting, I walked around feeling ashamed of myself. But I didn't change my actions. I simply quit the program. Why? Because shame is a terribly ineffective motivator. Shame doesn't bring change. What brings change are people standing together in solidarity, fighting for a mutual cause. What motivates someone is a *why*. It is an invitation to play an irreplaceable role in a story taking place in real time.

We've got reasons to be angry, right? I mean, in the year 2000, there were more CEOs at Fortune 500 companies named Michael than there were women CEOs in total.[6] No one's arguing that there's not a very real problem. But if all we do is wag our fingers and bang our fists, change will continue to occur a snail's pace. We need *massive* change *now*. And men play a crucial part in making that happen.

> We need *massive* change *now*. And men play a crucial part in making that happen.

One of my pet peeves is when people complain but don't offer a solution. I'm a question asker. I am curious. I joke that I'm nosy as hell. But, at the core, it's simply because I want to know why things are the way they are. When I see an injustice or a situation that isn't fair, I am compelled to speak out. But I want to be careful to speak out *and* offer a solution. Otherwise, what's the difference between speaking out and complaining?

When we point out disparities, especially when it comes to systemic issues like gender inequality, and we don't offer a solution, it can often (almost always) come across as finger-pointing. It becomes the blame game.

Instead of being invited into the conversation, men are often pushed out. They've become targets of our conversations instead of active participants. And if we want change at the grassroots level— which we do—we've got to include *everyone* in the conversation. Without men, we're missing 50 percent of the solution.

Men receive their own set of toxic messages. This isn't a book on the plight of the working dad, but unpacking most men's internal conflict may help us shed some light on solutions. Solutions for mothers, for fathers. *Real* solutions for families. Understanding where men are coming from will inform our course of action and, in the meantime, give us a level of empathy for what it means to be a man in America.

We need men to be in the rooms of change with us. To invite men into the conversation and avoid shaming them into silence, we've got to dig beneath our anger and find a passion that unites. A passion that inspires, not ostracizes. A passion that includes, not rejects.

So, how can we invite men into the conversation about gender equality so that we can work together toward a better tomorrow?

I'd love to return to that conversation I had with my colleague back in 2007, when I'd returned from my "vacation," aka my maternity leave. Instead of setting out to crucify him for his ignorance, I could have invited him into the conversation—explaining to him what I had actually experienced and how we can best work together in this new normal. He didn't know what he didn't know.

That's why carrying an invitation to long-term engagement in this critical conversation is necessary. Writing books, holding conferences, and doing one-off trainings is not getting the job done.

We need to include men in the cause. It can't be just a women's cause—it's got to be a *human* cause. We have to talk to men about our experiences and the experiences of others, and we need to learn how to do it in a way that doesn't scream, "This is your fault!" but communicates instead, "This affects all of us, and we need your help." I'm not sure how we've intuitively missed this step for so many years, but it's the way we're going to GSD, as my mom says.

PATERNITY LEAVE

Let's get super practical here. There is one real, practical, and tangible way men can improve conditions for working moms. It's so simple, it's laughable: *Men, take your paternity leave. All of it.* And if you don't have paternity leave, fight for it.

I remember when John went back to work the day after I had Landon. His superiors actually applauded him. Gave him an ovation. Something along the lines of, "He just had a baby, and look how committed he is to his job!" The clapping and the rah-rah-rahing made me want to barf. If you'll remember, this was around the same time that my producer was telling me that I wasn't giving my "best look" at work, so you'll forgive me if I didn't join in the adulation.

When I asked John why he didn't take any paternity leave, he was brutally honest. "I didn't want to take it," he said. "I don't like newborn life. I don't like changing diapers, getting no sleep, and a kid screaming in the background. I think most men feel that way."

"John," I said, "how are you and I supposed to join together in this fight with that kind of attitude? Do you think moms *enjoy* any of that, either?"

"Yeah," he said, "I thought you enjoyed it."

I realized then that I hadn't done two things I should have done in early parenthood: (1) While I loved my infants wildly, I hadn't honestly expressed how much I disliked so many aspects of early motherhood. (2) I hadn't asked for him to stay and help. I hadn't made it seem like his presence and participation were important—or even necessary. After all, I was the one with the milk, right?

I also had no idea how paternity leaves offer incredible intrinsic and extrinsic outcomes. In an article for the *New York Times*, finance and tech guru Nathaniel Popper discusses his own experience.[7] His first son was born in 2012. The only paid time off he was offered was a week of vacation that he had to work to earn. At the time, paternity leave was out of the question.

Fast-forward five years to 2017 and the birth of his second son. Nathaniel was offered ten fully paid weeks of paternity leave, which he took all of. "Those first two months of life with a newborn were just as sleepless as they had been the first time around," Nathaniel writes. "But there were fewer fights and less resentment, and my wife got to go back to her own work more quickly."

Nathaniel also notes that long after his paternity leave was over, he noticed a difference in how he related to his second son. "To this day he regularly calls out for me in the night in a way that my first son rarely did. And when I am with him, I feel a certain intangible sense of ease that has only come more recently with my older son."

Studies confirm that Nathaniel's experience is not happenstance. A 2019 paper by Richard Petts, Chris Knoester, and Jane Waldfogel said that even nine years later, children whose fathers took at least two weeks of paternity leave felt closer to their dads than kids with fathers who didn't take paternity leave.[8]

When a father takes paternity leave, his choice doesn't just improve the outcomes for the father and the child, but for the mother as well. An article on the McKinsey website says, "Studies also show that a father's increased involvement in baby care can mitigate maternal postpartum-depression outcomes. A study of how paternity leave affects maternal postpartum depression showed that a lack of paternal involvement was a significant predictor of the intensity of depressive symptoms."[9]

Despite the overwhelming evidence of its benefits, the Department of Labor reports that most American men take only a few days of leave after the birth or adoption of a child.[10]

Men don't take paternity leave for two main reasons. First, they aren't offered paid paternity leave. In the United States, very few companies offered paid paternity *or* maternity leave. We'll unpack this later in greater detail, but we need men to band together and demand they be given the same leave options. In 2016, a new father brought a class action suit against JPMorgan Chase after he was denied a sixteen-week paid parental leave on the grounds that he wasn't the "primary caregiver," a benefit that is extended to its female employees.

The dad won. "As part of the proposed settlement, the company will take steps to ensure that its policy is administered in a gender-neutral way. And it will create a $5 million fund to compensate up to about 5,000 fathers who were shortchanged in the past."[11]

CNN and Estée Lauder have recently settled similar suits.

One battle at a time, we can win this fight.

Second, taking paternity leave is risky, both financially and professionally. Adrienne Schweer of the Bipartisan Policy Center's Task Force on Paid Family Leave says, "There is a stigma to being away from work, especially for men...Men tend not to take leave because they see the impact it has on a woman's career and earnings, they see how the absence causes someone else to pick up additional work to fill in and they don't feel their leadership supports them in taking the leave."[12]

Globally, the average paid maternity leave is twenty-nine weeks, and the average paid paternity leave is sixteen weeks.[13] The United States, however, is one of only three countries in the world that does not have federally mandated parental leave, and the vast majority of American businesses do not offer it.[14]

In the summer of 2022, I traveled to Europe with my family and was blown away by the number of fathers actively engaged in child-rearing, particularly in Paris. Fathers pushing their young children in strollers, fathers lunching with their children, fathers riding the subway with their kids, fathers caring for their kids. It seemed so…natural. And I loved it.

When I posted about it on my social media, I received a flood of comments such as "one of the many reasons we decided to move from the U.S. to Europe" and "this is normal in Europe."

Normal? Wow.

Then I received a message from a friend of mine, an American journalist, who said this: "Paula, you know my husband works remotely for a French company. He had SIX months of paternity leave. He went back to work AFTER ME. Most of his European friends have the same if not more time. Speaking from personal experience, it shifts the dynamics of parenting when you're given time to parent together like that. Not having paternity leave changes the dynamic in such a crazy way…forever. I am so grateful my husband was able to be home and with us. He is just amazing."

That right there is the power of paternity leave. Paternity leave shifts parenting dynamics.

We're going to talk later about actions corporate America must take to adapt to a changed labor force and market. And creating safety for employees who need to care for young kids and/or adult parents is at the top of that list.

Before Elon Musk took over Twitter, its former CEO announced[15] that he would be taking a few weeks of paternity leave when he and his wife had their baby. His announcement was met with reactions ranging from commendation to condemnation. Of note, Twitter offered up to twenty weeks of paid paternity leave. In light of what could potentially have been five months of investing in a new life, I was bummed by the CEO's choice to only take a "couple of weeks" off from work.

Some lauded the CEO for taking any leave at all, while others, like me, were left a bit disappointed. We need men to approach paternity leave fully committed to being equal partners in all phases of their child's life.

One of the things I'm committed to doing at CARRY Media is shining a light on companies that are doing it right—not just calling out the ones that aren't. We have a segment in our weekly newsletter, *The CARRY ALL*, called "The ShoutOut," where we feature organizations, companies, and brands doing right for working moms and parents.

In one particular edition, we featured international conglomerate Deloitte for their "new and improved parental leave policy that gives equal terms for all parents." Their CEO, Anders Dons, elaborated on Deloitte's new policy, sharing a heartfelt LinkedIn post cautioning followers to "Never ever cheat yourself, no matter what, take your leave and your time with your kids."[16] He then posted a photo about why he wished he'd taken it.

He wrote this: "I am so proud of my five lovely kids. My first twins, Tobias & Matilde, and my second set of twins, Nikolaj & Sara, and Alberte. What I am not proud of is that I hardly took any parental leave. I left it to my lovely wife, Lise. Never ever cheat yourself, no matter what, take your leave and your time with your kids.

"I have for years promised myself to work hard for changing the culture in our society to get to an equal playing ground. In Deloitte we want to push for an equal distribution of parental leave because that is the single most effective tool to improve gender equality in the workplace. That's why we're introducing a new and improved parental leave policy that gives equal terms for all parents in Deloitte. More specifically, we are giving fathers and co-parents 24 weeks of paid leave—thereby putting them on par with mothers. Let's get it right for the next generation."

I love that last sentence: *Let's get it right for the next generation.* We all say that we want our kids to have it better than we did. So let's make good on our word and do something different when it comes to inviting men into the conversation about gender equality at home and at work.

Stories like Reddit co-founder Alexis Ohanian's give me hope. You may have heard of his wife, tennis superstar Serena Williams. Alexis, who still worked at Reddit at the time of his daughter's birth, was able to take sixteen weeks of paid paternity leave, which turned out to be a double blessing, since Serena came very close to death following complications from an emergency C-section.

Alexis says, "I couldn't imagine going through that as a husband and having to decide or even think for a second about choosing between your wife and your career. That is an inhumane choice to expect someone to make in a modern society."[17]

With Serena bedbound for six weeks following multiple surgeries, most of the childcare duties fell to Alexis, who had previously never even held a baby. "I learned how to do a diaper and I learned how to do all these things and just get comfortable with this tiny little person that I was now responsible for."

As a result of his crash course in hands-on parenting, Alexis has become a vocal proponent of men taking paternity leave and is using his voice to advocate for a national paid family leave in the United States.

Alexis predicts a culture change is coming. He says, "What social media has unlocked is more and more boring, everyday examples of dads in the role [of caretaker]. Just dadding, not babysitting, but just dadding, and that's an important shift."

EXTENDING AN INVITATION

My friend's daughter recently came home from school upset. Her mom asked her why she was upset—a mama knows when one of her own is "off." It's part of our superpowers.

"These boys were mean to me," her daughter said.

"Tell me what happened."

"Our teacher told us to clean up. If we didn't clean up in five minutes, the entire class would lose recess time the next day."

"Okay."

"The boys weren't cleaning. They were just sitting on the reading rug. So I went over there and said, 'The teacher told us we all have to clean up. But only the girls are cleaning. We need your help, or we're going to lose recess time.'"

One of the taller boys rolled his eyes and looked at my friend's daughter. "Who died and made you queen," he said. "No wonder you have no friends. You're bossy."

(When is the last—or first—time you heard a man described as *bossy*?)

My friend stopped what she was doing and looked at her daughter. "If a boy had told him to help clean, what do you think this kid would have done?"

The daughter shrugged. "I don't know. He wouldn't have called him bossy."

"You're probably right," the mom said.

The daughter thought for a minute. "That's true." She thought some more. "That's not really fair. How come a girl can't say the same things a boy can say without being bossy?"

The next day my friend's daughter came home from school. "I told that boy not to call me bossy again," she announced.

The mom, worried her daughter had rained down terror on the kid, pressed for more details.

"I just told him that it wasn't fair to call a girl bossy for just telling the truth," her daughter said. "It's not nice. I said, 'You don't call boys bossy!' Then we decided to make a rule in our class: *Bossy* is a bad word."

I thought about my friend's story. I want to be more like that daughter. She went straight to the offending man. She stated the facts. She shared the struggle clearly and unemotionally. Then she invited him to help her in a better way forward. Together, those two third graders changed the culture of an entire classroom in under five minutes.

Just think what we'd be able to do if we carried an invitation to this conversation to our offices, to our male friendships, to our male family members, to all the men in our life—our sons, sons-in-law, grandsons, husbands.

The earlier we can extend this invitation and share the conversation, the faster we will be able to create solutions and help them be a part of the change.

Landon is eight and has his first crush. I asked Landon, "What is she like?"

"She runs really fast at the playground," he said.

"That's impressive," I said. "What does she look like?"

And he said, "She looks like you, Mommy."

And I said, "Is that why you like her?"

He smiled his smug little smile and nodded, and my heart exploded and melted all at the same time.

Gosh, I love my kids—but I have a massive crush on my boys. They do something to my heart. But because of how much I love them, it's my responsibility to educate them. To talk to them early and often about what it's like to be on the other side of the gender coin. To empower them to stand up for their sister, for girls at school, and, one day, for their partners. These conversations happen often in my house already. Granted, I need to rein Land-o in, because when we talk about standing up for people, his first reaction is to kick the bad person "in the balls."

Ladies, we can't push men out of parenting, push men out of housework, and push men out of this conversation and expect our outcomes to improve. We need their help. I'm not at all saying the responsibility lies on us…or that this is our cross to bear. But it would go a long way if we would carry an invitation for them to partner with us in saying, "Hey, this isn't fair. Will you help me create some solutions?"

TEAMWORK

We all need help. We need to communicate with our spouses in order to be better partners. You need a team to raise kids. That's why I so greatly admire single moms. The US has the highest rate of children living in single-parent households, according to the Pew Research Center.[18] My co-writer on this book, Holly, is a single mom of three. As is my editor, Daisy. They are true superheroes!

I love what author and radio talk show host Gary Chapman told me about what it's like for single parents: "It is a major role to raise a child and work, and typically a single mom has to work. That's when I say to extended family members, 'She needs help. Ask how you can help.'"

I had the honor of interviewing Chapman for this book. Anybody who's been around me knows that his book *The Five Love Languages* is literally the most transformative book in my life. I loved hearing him talk about how parents not only need to know each other's love language, but they also have to see themselves as a team—people with different gifts and interests, but still a team:

> One of the best things we can do for our children is give them a model of a mom and a dad who love each other, who are looking out for each other, who are there for each other, who are trying to help each other, working together as a team, loving, supporting, and caring for each other. When we don't do that, and it's not intentional most of the time, when we let the children be the focus of our family, we drift apart in the marriage.

It's so easy to unintentionally drift apart. Especially when it's a busy season in a household, like it is in ours.

Caroline is playing travel volleyball, and JJ is playing travel basketball, with both of their tournaments often a few hours away. One particular weekend, JJ's games collided with Caroline's tournament.

Our plan? Take two separate cars to JJ's game so that John and Caroline could leave right after it ended for Atlanta, where Caroline's volleyball tournament began the next morning, and I could bring the boys home.

We had it all planned out and I was so proud of us!

I'd asked Landon to take Caroline's luggage to the car before we went to JJ's game. I remember thinking at the time, *I should make sure Land-o got her bag in the trunk. What a cluster that would be if the bag got left behind by mistake.*

Before we left, John asked if everything and everyone was where they needed to be. "We're all set!" I confirmed.

All was going according to our magnificent plan. I took Caroline and Landon to JJ's game, and afterward, John and I traded kids and cars.

Caroline opened the trunk and looked around. "Where's my bag?"

You see, Landon *had* taken Caroline's luggage to the car, but had failed to actually put it in the car. It was just feet away, sitting in the garage.

John had to drive over an hour out of his way to pick up the luggage, defeating the effectiveness of our best-laid plans and causing a whole lot of stress and anxiety before a big tournament.

John, because he is an actual saint, didn't lay blame. "Sorry, honey," I told him. "I forgot to double-check for that bag."

Great teams and partners communicate, and they also admit their mistakes. But even the best teams have their issues. John and I struggled earlier in our marriage, even separating for a while, and we're so grateful we stuck it out.

But if there's anything out there that will drive us to divorce, it's dinner.

After all these years of marriage, we still fight, and our biggest disagreement happens to be over cooking dinner.

John doesn't like cooking and says he's not good at cooking. He doesn't expect me to cook. However, I don't like cooking or think I'm particularly good at it, either.

This is what we call a stalemate.

I recently asked John about this during a spirited and playful debate on the subject.

"So, when's the last time you planned a meal besides going through the drive-thru?" I asked. "Like *really* planned it. Shopped for it, cooked it, prepped it."

"I don't know," John said.

"So, is that fair to put that on me, though? Because, you know, I'll just do it. But I'm bad at it and I hate it and I resent you for it."

"My hope is that you'll just get over it," John told me with his playful grin.

"It's been twenty-five years. I'm not getting over it."

"Yeah, I figured it would just go away eventually."

I'm not lying—we've gone to therapy because of this. But at least we can still talk openly with one another about this.

"This is where I think we can partner a lot better," I told John. "I think you are a good vocational partner in supporting me pursuing my dreams. But I don't feel like you're a great domestic partner. You're getting better. You're a great dad. But I still feel like the backstop and the goalie, like I have to plan and make the kids' appointments. I know the kids' teachers' names. You don't."

"There are certain things that you're just much better at," John said. "And I just kind of let you stay in your lane. There are certain things that I do. I'm not asking you to go out there and mow the lawn and take care of the dock. There are certain things I just do. I never ask you to take the trash out."

"I take the trash out."

"When was the last time you went to the dump? To the recycling bin? I go there twice a week."

"True, but it's different," I said. "Like the daily stuff—the cooking, the mental load of 'what are we going to have for dinner?' gives me just about more stress than anything else. You know this is causing me stress. And I've told you also, conversely, that there's nothing hotter than you cooking."

"What did I do tonight? I grilled that chicken."

"I prepped everything else, and I even marinated the chicken. You just literally grilled it."

"So you're demeaning the grill?"

"But even coming up with dinner. 'What are we going to have tonight? Do we have the ingredients?' I had to go to two stores to get it. You know what I mean? You don't have to worry about any of that."

"We should hire a cook," John joked.

I'm the first to admit that sometimes, ladies, we're the ones who drop the ball. But sometimes, men, we just need you to step up to the plate. And that might include the dinner plate!

WHAT NOW?

Ninety-eight hours.

That's the number of hours the average working mom puts in each week when family responsibilities are included, according to a study commissioned by Welch's.

Moms, no wonder we're *fried*.

This work we put in outside of our jobs is often referred to as the "second shift." And it disproportionally falls on moms.

Eve Rodsky wrote a best-selling book about it called *Fair Play* and turned it into a documentary on how we can best partner with our partners on the division of labor.[19]

My immediate thoughts about this were *I shouldn't have to even ask!* and *John isn't doing me a favor by grabbing milk at the grocery store. This is his responsibility, too.*

Ladies, the mental juggle of trying to figure out what you need for whom and when you need it can be exhausting. It just never ends!

In the *Fair Play* documentary, there was a statistic that made me laugh, because it's often true in my household: 46 percent of moms say their husbands stress them out more than their children.

But it's no laughing matter that we have to partner better—at work and at home. Ladies, do not diminish how exhausting this is for you. I know it's easier to just do it ourselves sometimes. However, these issues are real and matter to us—partners divorce over the sponge left in the sink. We know it's not just a sponge. So for our own mental sanity, we must talk about it and come to some resolutions.

Below you'll find a list to get you started. By no means is it comprehensive. And what works for one person might not work for another. I could write hundreds of pages about this topic alone, but this is a good jumping-off point to get the conversation going.

At Home

Eve Rodsky suggests opening the conversation with asking your partner what the division of labor looked like in your house growing up. Was the workload divided? What were you responsible for as a child?

- Is there a specific point in the day, or during the week, when it's hard to juggle the shifting parts in the home?
- What's one thing your partner could take off your plate that would be a game-changer for you?
- Do you ever feel it is easier to execute a task yourself? If so, why? How does your partner feel about this?
- When it comes to your time, do you believe an hour taking your child to the pediatrician's office is just as valuable as an hour spent in the office? Discuss why or why not.
- In her article "Splitting Chores Can Be Unfair. Here's How to Do It Equitably," Allie Volpe gave a list of ways spouses can help with work around the house, including not making assumptions about who will do the task, and remembering that the kids can do chores, too. "The way to encourage everyone in the house to contribute to chores involves getting all parties to 'own' their tasks."[20]

At Work

Author and researcher Joanne Lipman recommends the following practical steps we can all take in the workplace on behalf of moms:

- Acknowledge and give credit to men who work and speak on our behalf.
- Be respectful when expressing your frustration or disappointments in how working moms are treated.

- Proactively consider asking for raises (as noted earlier, men are four times more likely to ask for a raise than women, and when women do ask, they ask for 30 percent less than men).
- Find women in leadership and ask them to put their hands up on your and other women's behalf.
- Raise the issues at a neutral time, not when a guy has just said something dumb.
- If you have a women's employee resource group, invite men to a meeting—but not just a blanket invitation. For example, every senior woman could invite one senior man. The men can listen in, ask questions, and participate.
- Don't forget that it isn't just women who should bring up an issue; we shouldn't put the onus on the marginalized person in the room to educate the person in power. The onus should be on the leadership, especially when you have male leadership. I know of some male CEOs who have gone on "listening tours" where they go out for dinner or coffee with a group of women or other marginalized employees and ask them to explain what their experience is like at the company.

CHAPTER NINE

CARRYING CORPORATE CHANGE

I am hard pressed to understand why we don't consider being a mother actual work. We are literally raising the next generation of human beings... of employees...of leaders.

—Rocki Howard, Chief People and Equity Officer,

The Mom Project

Be kind to yourself. As women, we are often our own worst critics. Take the pressure off yourself to be perfect at all your roles. Also, get help if you need it. It took pretty significant postpartum anxiety for me to admit that I needed help. Prioritizing your mental health is always worth it.

—Meg, senior accounts manager and mom of two

I met up with some of my high school girlfriends recently for a ridiculous weekend of laughing, reminiscing (aka looking at our high school yearbooks), and bad dietary decisions. My girlfriend Michelle is part of that group. We graduated together in the great Jackson Baptist class of 1993. All twenty-five of us.

For the last twenty years, Michelle has had, in my opinion, a dream employer for a working mom. Her two kids are nineteen and twenty now, but when they were little, Michelle was able to spend most of her time working a flex schedule. Prior to working at a cancer clinic together, Michelle had worked for her boss at another organization for five years. Altogether, Michelle has worked for her employer the entire time she's been a mother.

When we were hanging out, I made a point to ask Michelle how she was able to get her sweet scheduling scenario. "I quit," Michelle said. "Or, I tried to. When I had my first child, I told her that I couldn't work five full days in the office anymore."

At that point, Michelle had been working for her boss for five years.

"What did she say?" I asked.

"She said, 'I'll let you do whatever you want. You don't have to come into work.' She promised I could come in once a week to pick up paperwork and check in, but that I could work from wherever I wanted the rest of the week. She let me keep this schedule until the kids were in middle school. By then, I was ready to come back full-time anyway. She has allowed me to be there for my kids whenever I needed to be."

I was stunned.

"But even now, if I need to take time off," Michelle added, "she allows it without making me feel guilty. She knows I'll get the work done."

"How do you feel about your boss?" I asked.

"I'd do anything for her. My sense of loyalty to her and the organization is limitless, because they allowed me to raise my kids and keep my career."

Michelle's story is an anomaly. I don't share it to rub our noses in how much more understanding her boss has been compared to ours, but to illustrate two distinctions: (1) Working moms can get anything done given the right schedule. (2) When employers support moms and families, everybody wins. Families get the investment they need, and employers get a loyal employee.

Sue Campbell, coauthor of *The Parental Leave Playbook: 10 Touchpoints to Transition Smoothly, Strengthen Your Family, and Continue Building Your Career*, told me, "Becoming a parent is our most overlooked leadership development opportunity! Companies that don't support working parents are missing out on some of the best workers around. When well supported, parents are efficient, effective, and amazing at prioritization. They are also fiercely loyal to employers who they feel have their back and create an environment where they can thrive at work and at home."[1]

Working moms don't come with a list of unreasonable demands. In Sue's words, we just need corporate America to have our backs in the systemic fight for moms.

I love sharing this.

We're always looking for compelling stories at CARRY Media, and we came across one on LinkedIn. It was a post from a guy by the name of Jon

> "When well supported, parents are efficient, effective, and amazing at prioritization. They are also fiercely loyal to employers who they feel have their back and create an environment where they can thrive at work and at home."

Zacharias—co-founder of an agency called GR0.[2] His post mentioned that he hired a mom who had never worked outside of the home and didn't have a fancy resume, and he wound up hitting the jackpot. He wrote:

> Sure, sometimes:
> - Her camera is off during Zoom calls.
> - She works nights instead of mornings.
> - She can't make it to meetings because her kids need her.

But he went on to say she is an empathetic leader and beloved by the team—his number one employee, in fact!

Her "mommy gap" didn't matter.

Corporate America, take note. Measure the measurables. And Jon, thank you for taking the risk and showing that there's no greater employee than a mom.

I believe we've got to take this fight to the streets—to Wall Street and every other street and internet highway that houses companies and businesses all over our country. We need corporations to begin making changes now that support working moms and families.

Why? Because our well-being, our mental health, and our *lives* are at stake.

What can corporations do about it? Here are four potential solutions based on what's already working for working moms and families in other countries as well as what companies are doing to celebrate, champion, and advocate for moms:

1. Offer flexible work options.
2. Provide affordable childcare.

3. Help negotiate parental benefits for employees.
4. Establish more moms in positions of leadership.

OFFER FLEXIBLE WORK OPTIONS

I was talking to my friend and fellow working mama Laura just the other day about the importance of flexibility in a work schedule. Her full-time in-office job went completely remote during the COVID-19 quarantine of 2020. She spent the next year and a half working from home and being more productive than ever on every front—work *and* home.

She said, "I can be on a call until five thirty p.m. and then make it to the soccer field at six. Why would *anyone* ever want to go back to 'normal'?"

Laura wasn't the only working parent (or working person, for that matter) who felt this way.

Another friend of mine who works in New York City says she cried when she received her return-to-office memo. It was not an option. It was an ultimatum. Get back to the job or you'll lose yours.

The Great Recession became the great "SheCession" in 2020 as moms were asked to carry it all plus some more when schools and daycare centers across the country shut their doors due to the pandemic.

Since women are the default care providers, all the education and childcare duties fell squarely on our laps. Not for the first time in America's history, many women in dual-income households were forced to leave their positions, even temporarily, to meet the needs at home while their higher-paid male partner remained on the job.

Economists warn that the SheCession could not only move us backward in terms of equal pay and representation on executive boards, but the American economy itself could be adversely affected, and, as Jennifer Glass told us earlier, 70 percent of women are expected to be the primary breadwinners at some point in their children's time at home.

I loved how Carly Martinetti and her team at Notably said a resounding no to returning to the office in a viral LinkedIn post.

"We're staying remote. I don't care how early or how late you work—As long as you're on top of your responsibilities. Because I'm running a company. Not a daycare center."[3]

Mary Beth Ferrante is the founder of WRK/360, a training and development platform helping to create and improve the culture of workplaces for women, working parents, and caregivers. In another viral LinkedIn post, she gave working moms permission for a permanent out-of-office responder in light of the pandemic: "Ask for support, deadline extensions, and empathy. Try even setting up your own 'out of office' to remind others that we are still in fact working during a pandemic and juggling care and work is already hard enough during the best of times."[4]

The juggle? Leaders like Mary Beth and Carly get it.

The People Have Spoken

While the pandemic forced millions of parents out of the workforce, what it also did was empower us to say "no more." We don't want to go back to the old ways of working, which includes the "traditional" nine-to-five job. Those rigid hours kept many moms on the sidelines to begin with.

In the past, corporations could demand that employees show

up in the office for a solid forty or more weekly hours and still attract talent. That's not the case anymore.

The Milwaukee-based law firm Gimbel, Reilly, Guerin & Brown was celebrated in a recent *Milwaukee Journal Sentinel* article for their flexible workplace policies like their refusal to track paid time off (PTO). Erin Strohbehn, partner at Gimbel, Reilly, Guerin & Brown, said, "We don't track PTO anymore…As long as you get your work done, you have flexibility. You take the time off that you need."[5]

She said that as a smaller law firm, they can't compete with the salaries larger firms have. But if they're a better place to work, they will attract employees who value flexibility. And that's exactly what people are looking for. Listen to these numbers from the *Wall Street Journal*: "Ninety-five percent of people surveyed want flexible hours, compared with 78% of workers who want location flexibility, according to a new report from Future Forum, a consortium focused on reimagining the future of work led by Slack Technologies Inc."[6]

Ninety-five percent.

The people have spoken! And why should companies care about this? Sue Campbell predicts that companies will be left in the dust if they don't start listening. "Millennials and Gen Z have very different expectations of employers than previous generations," she told me.[7] "Companies who don't implement family-friendly policies will face a serious recruiting and retention crisis—and soon."

Listen Up, Employers
Offering remote work and hybrid workweeks aren't your only options. Countries like France have been recognized for implementing the

thirty-five-hour workweek, and employees in Scandinavian countries like Norway and Denmark work an average of thirty-three hours per week. One country that has not been historically recognized in the fight for flexible policies is Denmark, coming in just shy of thirty hours with a standard twenty-nine-hour workweek to make it the lowest weekly hours worked in any developed country.[8]

One shoutout we gave in our CARRY Media newsletter went out to the 70 companies and 3,300 employees in the United Kingdom for having the you-know-what to pilot a four-day workweek. It was a 6-month trial, monitored by researchers. And guess what? It was a success! Good for employers (average revenue was up) and good for employees, who reported lower levels of stress, burnout, etc. Some employers even called it "transformative."

Getting more done in less time? That's a working mom's bread and butter.

> Getting more done in less time? That's a working mom's bread and butter.

But we have to band together to bring about change.

Unfortunately, I've found during this reporting process that not many employees feel safe raising their hands and saying they're having challenges at home or work.

Leslie Forde, founder of Mom's Hierarchy of Needs, told me that less than 3 percent of employees say they're able to be honest with their manager about what they need, according to their most recent study.

So, as an employee, what can you do about it? The experts I spoke with say to do the following:

- Explore any existing employee resource groups (ERGs) at your workplace. Seek out other parents and caregivers. Companies are more receptive to listening to employee needs via these groups.
- Inquire about any current efforts your employer is taking toward family-friendly policies.
- Champion a companywide survey to capture the voices of other employees.

Business owners and executives, offering workday flexibility will require a high level of trust from you. It may also require a little extra strategizing to align your calendar with your overall organizational goals. But we are worth it. With employers fighting to support us at work and at home, working mamas can reenter or remain in the workforce, serving to benefit our entire country.

PROVIDE AFFORDABLE CHILDCARE

The pandemic revealed the ineffectiveness of more than one American system. But maybe chief among the pack is our nation's formula for childcare. It's not working for anyone—not mothers, not hourly caregivers, and not companies.

The piecemeal solutions that our families, friends, private daycares, and companies have created are no longer enough—we need larger, universal, more comprehensive policies to address the childcare crisis in our country…and we need them *yesterday*.

It may be tempting for corporate America to examine our country's childcare problem and say, "How is that my responsibility? It's a parent's job to figure that out on their own." But as an article from *Business Insider* points out, "When childcare infrastructure is not in place, or childcare costs go beyond income, it becomes a problem for all of us. When people can't afford kids, they have less kids. Low birth rates can cause labor shortages that will shrink our economic output. If you own a company, less people in the labor pool means less ability to grow."[9]

Next time corporations and employers say it's not their problem or your friend who doesn't have kids echoes that sentiment, show them that quote. Or tell them this: "Poor childcare = low birth rates = labor shortage = economic doom."

We *all* need to be involved in helping to solve this problem.

If your company can't afford to offer full-time childcare or family leave, get creative, like the African American Breastfeeding Network (AABN) did. This Milwaukee-based nonprofit is led by working mom Dalvery Blackwell, whose experience working for a family-friendly organization as a young mom compelled her to go above and beyond for the working moms on her team.

The AABN is permitting their peer counselors and lactation consultants to set their own schedules and bring their children to work. They also offer childcare during networking events.

"If you support working women and create a family-friendly environment, you're going to have an employee who's happy, who comes to work, who's very productive, who's enjoyable to work with—even if she took every Friday off to pick up her child from school," Blackwell said.

Supported Mothers = Productive Mothers

Imagine a world where going back to work after maternity leave didn't also mean leaving your baby. One company is doing just that: Brains on Fire (BOF), a full-service branding agency based in Greenville, South Carolina. It has a program called

Babies at Work. The policy affords employees the option to bring their babies to the office with them until they are six months old or mobile.

"We wanted to ensure our moms felt safe and cared for while nursing and growing a human," co-president and CEO Brandy Amidon said. "We, as a company, understood those first few months of a baby's life are so formative in laying a healthy foundation for mom and baby. We wanted our moms to have the choice to continue working and not feel pressured to decide between being a mom or having a career or daycare. An added plus, our team *loved* having babies in the office. We truly felt invested in our BOF babies' success for a lifetime after we'd played, cried and laughed together at work."

Pretty amazing, right? And the last time we checked, Brains on Fire was hiring.

There are other inspiring examples of companies helping to find creative solutions to childcare, like fresh baby food startup Once Upon a Farm, which is the kind of employer that makes their working moms *rave* about them online. A LinkedIn post went viral when their director of sales, Kristin O'Connell, shared how the company hired her while she was six and a half months pregnant, paid her full salary for four months while she was out on maternity leave, and didn't prorate those months she was out on her bonus.[10] Once Upon a Farm even offered to expense the cost of the Milk Stork service so Kristin could feed her baby while she traveled for work.

"Once Upon a Farm knows that it's worth it to hire the right person and that their investment in me will be paid back to the business multifold with the work that I do," Kristin wrote. "A supported mother is a productive one."

I couldn't agree more.

Another such company is CPA Moms, which, according to their website, sees moms as the "most overlooked, untapped resource of dedicated professionals."[11] Founder Mayumi Young's story and CPA Moms' values and culture left our jaws on the floor and our hands in the air.

Their company values and culture statement says, "CPA MOMS empowers talented CPA mompreneurs who want to have both a firm and a family, provides entrepreneurs with accurate & affordable accounting & tax services nationwide, and puts family first." Their vision and mission statement says, "We take care of the moms, so they can take care of you. At CPA MOMS, working moms no longer have to choose between having a firm and family."

Why aren't more companies following examples like this?

Societies Should Support Families

The brokenness of our childcare system isn't a new issue. We've even solved this problem before. During World War II, when women were mobilized to run American factories with their men at war, it was quickly recognized that someone had to look after the children. The political will was there, and the Lanham Act led to a government-run childcare program that was up and running within weeks. *Weeks.* Yes, here in America, the government took charge of a hugely successful national, high-quality childcare program. It will cost money. But if it was essential to keeping our economy afloat then, it is essential now.[12]

The US may have forgotten about its once-successful childcare program, but other countries have not.

Typical two-year-olds in Denmark attend childcare during the day, where they are guaranteed a spot, and their parents pay no more than 25 percent of the cost. That guaranteed spot will remain until the children are in after-school care at age ten. If their parents choose to stay home or hire a nanny, the government helps pay for that, too.[13]

As mentioned earlier, in the US, it costs more to send a toddler to daycare for a year than it does to send a college student to an in-state university for the same amount of time. Two-year-olds in the US are far less likely to attend formal childcare than children of the same age in other "rich" countries. If parents are able to budget for daycare and they're able to secure a spot on the roster, they'll pay full price: an average of $1,100 per month per child.

> In the US, it costs more to send a toddler to daycare for a year than it does to send a college student to an in-state university for the same amount of time.

Remember Jennifer Glass's research findings that being a parent essentially makes us less happy than non-parents? That's largely because parents can't afford to raise kids in this country. On the *Life Examined* podcast, she said, "What worries me is we've created a new social compact…The costs of children are privatized, but the benefits of children are socialized."[14]

What does she mean? Parents pay to raise their children. Society benefits from those children. As parents, we're investing the majority of our income into childcare, after-school care, medical care, furthering education, training, and so on. And who reaps the benefits? The parents? Um, no. In the same podcast episode, she said, "An employer gets this great employee who has been educated and trained by someone else's dollars, our tax base gets a nice big income tax off of that person, and then there's another payroll for Social Security and Medicare. All of that money is going to be disbursed both to people who had children and people who never had children."[15]

American voters, we need to elect officials who will help us catch up to what's happening in other developed nations—nations whose attitudes are "I am my brother's keeper." Nations that don't hesitate to put kids' and working parents' needs at the forefront of social issues. Nations that band together through government policy and private practice to support working parents. Societies that support families! Children are either our country's greatest natural resource… or they aren't.

We need wide-sweeping legislation that will create government-supported educational opportunities like the ones enjoyed by children in France at age two and in the UK and Scandinavia at age three. This does two things: It benefits working families and corporations, plus it helps our kids get an earlier start on cognitive development.

As consumers, we need to start supporting companies that provide on-site childcare services for their employees at a low or affordable rate, like Clif Bar & Company, Aflac, Goldman Sachs, Publix, Citi, Patagonia, and General Mills.[16] We're moms—we know how to reward what we want repeated!

HELP NEGOTIATE PARENTAL BENEFITS FOR EMPLOYEES

Corporate America, this is where you come in. You are in the position of influence. You hold the power to decrease levels of stress and anxiety that, left to run rampant, could have negative outcomes for your employees, their families, your business, and society. Your response to the news of an employee's pregnancy sets the tone for how the next few months will play out in your organization. You should be prepared with an informed response. An article in *Harvard Business Review* states, "A manager's initial reaction can shape perceptions of future treatment and therefore impact stress. While it is important to have a supportive tone at the time of disclosure, having an awareness of the company's parental benefits in advance can be especially helpful."[17]

Know your policy and know your limits. Don't make promises you can't keep that you'll have to walk back later. Don't act put out because your employee is perpetuating the whole race. We all got here the same way. In other words, *celebrate* your pregnant employees. You don't have to throw a baby shower (though that wouldn't hurt), but widen the lens of your response to the overall good coming your way. Remember, that pregnant employee is in the actual process of embracing or increasing her brainpower, capacity, and performance. This is good news for both of you.

Mamas, this is going to require some disclosure on your part. But when you're ready to share the news that you're pregnant, take it directly to your supervisor. Be clear and direct about your desired outcomes. Will you want a decrease in workload, or the workload to stay the same? How much leave would you like to take? We can sometimes assume that company policies apply across the board, but you never know what's possible unless you ask.

Setting the Standard

Some companies have spent years—even decades—prioritizing women in the workplace. One such organization is quintessential health and beauty brand Johnson & Johnson. Since its launch in 1886 (when eight of its fourteen original employees were women), equality has been at the forefront. To date, Johnson & Johnson has been named as one of the Top 100 Best Companies for Working

Moms by *Working Mother* magazine a whopping thirty-one times. And it's no secret as to why.

Aside from bringing some of the most-used health, beauty, and self-care items to the shelves of your favorite stores, Johnson & Johnson is setting the bar high for employers when it comes to caring for working moms. They not only pay for a full maternity leave (eight weeks for adoptive parents and up to seventeen weeks for moms who give birth), but Johnson & Johnson also boasts a ridiculously generous suite of benefits for working moms that make us wonder, *Why isn't this the standard?*

Another person putting mamas first is John Ruhlin, CEO of the Ruhlin Group and the creator of Giftology. His team consists mostly of moms with kids at home. "Moms are the most underrated workforce on the planet," John tells me. "We try to do things that make their life better outside of work hours, not just during work hours."

Some ways they're doing this?

- Covering biweekly housekeeping bills for their employees. They don't do a stipend because they know that money would get used on kids, groceries, and bills—so the moms pick the housecleaners and turn in receipts (which is *genius*).
- Paying for summer camps for employees' children—so the kids can have fun and the parents can catch a break.
- Sending family-oriented gifts to their employees and the employees' families year-round.

What's his retention rate with employees? Almost 100 percent. He says no one ever leaves because he treats his employees and their families so well. And where do most companies lose a lot of money? On employee turnover.

ESTABLISH MORE MOMS IN POSITIONS OF LEADERSHIP

Recently a social media campaign was started by a morning newsletter called *The Skimm* using the hashtag #ShowUsYourLeave. The post praised corporations like Pinterest, Estée Lauder, Motherly, and Pipette for having recently posted company paid leave policies on social media, and they challenged other businesses to do the same.[18]

How about a #ShowUsYourTable campaign? I want businesses and organizations to show us who is at the top levels of their companies. Not because I'm curious. We already know our corporate tables are dominated by white men. But because I want to hold companies accountable for their lack of diversity among leadership.

We've discussed at-length the need *for* and benefit *of* moms at the highest level of leadership within an organization, but it bears repeating: We need moms at the top. The changes required to protect and support American families won't come until moms have more of a voice in the cultural climate of businesses in this country.

Moms need to be in decision-making seats. In policy-informing seats. In seats of innovation and strategy. Moms deserve a seat at every table.

Behavior scientist, burnout survivor, and host of the *Overcoming Working Mom* podcast Jaqueline Kerr says that having women in leadership is the key to an American society that values working moms. "We need more female leaders in all levels of society," she says, "so that they can reshape social systems to prioritize well-being. We need diverse teams [and] objective performance criteria, including team well-being."

Another working mom who is a total hero of mine is Michelle Buelow, CEO and founder of Bella Tunno, an organization whose goal is to end child hunger in the US. "Women specifically need to be represented in leadership roles and C-suites and boardrooms, to show the next generation of female leaders what's possible," Michelle explains. "Currently, only 2 percent of women-owned companies get venture capital funding (private equity financing) and only 8 percent of Fortune 500 companies are run by women. You can't be what you can't see, so we need women in positions of influence and impact to change the statistics."

The CARRY Fund, which we're launching at CARRY, solely exists to push back against this narrative, creating a mompreneur fund that mentors and funds mompreneurs. Women overall get only 2 percent of the venture capital dollars, and women who are moms get even less!

Carrying corporate change is how, together, we get this done. It's how we find our new path forward.

Lean on Me

One company paving a new path is Constellation, a New York City–based digital marketing agency. CEO Diana Lee has built an incredible culture at her company that welcomes and elevates working moms. After thirty-plus years of working in the automotive industry, she wants to care for her employees so they can care for others. As an immigrant and a mother of three, she's walking the walk. Her company statistics represent this: 49 percent of employees are women, 60 percent of C-suite executives are people of color, and 20 percent of executives are women of color.

Anumita Steinberg wrote this on LinkedIn after her first day of work at Constellation: "My first day I witnessed my colleague participate in a leadership meeting with her 4-year-old coloring by her side. My CEO while speaking of work culture encouraged us to bring our kids whenever we wanted (mind blown!). I silently applauded the culture that created a safe environment for working moms to do what they needed to do unapologetically. This is exactly why we need more women in leadership positions. This was beyond your 'bring your kid to work day.' Diversity and inclusion at every touch point seems to be part of their DNA. Needless to say, I had a great first day!"[19]

Kendra Scott, CEO of the eponymous jewelry company and one of the few self-made female billionaires, is another woman in leadership who is doing it right. This includes making Mother's Day a paid company holiday. Inc.com reported, "Through the initiative, called 'Take the Time,' the company's retail and customer care teams working on Sunday will be paid an increased holiday rate, and the corporate office and distribution center will be closed on Monday in observance of the holiday."[20]

She is the mother of three boys and started her company when her first son was just three months old. Family has always come first to her and always will. In those early days of her company, nearly everyone in the office was a young mother, and they all saw it as a strength, not a liability. They wanted to have a career and a family.

"Our life is more than just work," Kendra said. "No one needs to choose between their work and their lives."[21]

With three thousand people on the payroll and 120 stand-alone stores, Kendra doesn't care when people work as long as they get the job done. At their headquarters, they have a gym at the front to prioritize health, and classes are held during the workday. Juice is served from the juice bar, and complimentary manicures are given during meetings with managers. When school is canceled or a babysitter calls out, moms can bring their kids to work. Children can stay at their mom's desk or in the playroom.

Kendra wrote a book titled *Born to Shine*, which I was happy to endorse. It's so good. I especially love this quote: "There is no way I would be who I am or where I am if I hadn't had a community of women to lean on and catch me when I was in the midst of a freefall, or to keep pushing me when the hill got steeper. You do not need to do it all and you CANNOT do it all."

TO THE DOUBTERS AND NAYSAYERS

It's easy to find pushback to these ideas, so before ending this chapter, let me address them head-on.

1. *"Why is this my problem? They're not my kids."*

   No, they're not your kids, but how we treat them and their families is all of our problem. Here's why: If we don't support families, we'll start to have fewer and fewer children. Fewer children = labor shortage. Labor shortage = economic crisis. That is certainly your problem and mine. Supporting families isn't just the right thing to do; it stands to benefit our entire society. And how we value families is the indication of how healthy a nation truly is.

Look at Europe, where the mentality is "I am my brother's keeper." Children aren't viewed as a valueless commodity. Children are their future, their respective country's great natural resource. So it benefits everyone to help raise the next generation.

2. *"I don't have kids...why should companies kowtow to families with their policies? What about me?"*

When companies value families, it naturally benefits everyone on the payroll because valuing the well-being of its employees becomes part of the company culture. At the end of the day, everyone on the payroll benefits.

I love what Leslie Forde, co-founder of Mom's Hierarchy of Needs, said about this: "The type of flexibility that will make a mother of young children successful in her career will also create a wonderful work environment for a twenty-five-year-old who wants to surf and have a dog. Family-friendly policies are flexible policies that allow people to live full lives while having full careers. Everybody wants that."

Also, why should parents be punished for furthering society? Someone has to procreate, or our future is nonexistent. Parenthood should be celebrated, not scrutinized. If we make it harder on families in the workforce, where parents make up 70 percent of the labor, we'll eventually have a labor shortage and economic doom.

Also, it's proven that parents are the most loyal employees when employers take care of them. Employee turnover is one of the costliest aspects of doing business.

3. *"I can't afford parental leave and childcare for my employees."*

This is a totally understandable response—it's costly to provide those benefits. However, when parents are taken care of in the workforce, they're beyond loyal. So the thing you spend the most on at your company—turnover—is essentially nonexistent if you take care of employees with families. I've interviewed a lot of companies who can't afford some of the pricier benefits, and they've gotten creative: allowing parents to set their own schedule (measuring the measurables), allowing parents to bring their kids to work when their babysitter bails or school is canceled, helping parents returning from family leave by allowing their babies in the office until they're mobile, and paying for housecleaning. These things make families feel seen and heard. Ask your employees what they want! I'd go so far as to say they'll give you some great ideas.

4. *"Why should I invest in moms?"*

Because if you want to GSD, you hire a mom. Becoming a mom gives you capabilities you didn't have before: empathy, courage, vision, leadership, efficiency, and so on—the kick-ass qualities you're desperately looking for in an employee. She's literally in front of you, or on the sidelines, waiting for the workplace to finally work for her. Don't make her choose between working and momming. Don't punish her for making sure the next generation arrives. Celebrate what she uniquely brings to the table, and she'll show up and show off.

TOP TEN WAY COMPANIES CAN CHAMPION WORKING MOMS:

1. Have moms on the board or as part of the decision-making team.
2. Offer work-from-home options or flexible schedules. Commit to measuring the measurables.
3. Provide childcare stipends or reimbursement support.
4. Eliminate pay gaps.
5. Establish sponsorship programs geared at training and equipping mothers to lead.
6. Create family-friendly policies and enforce them. And leaders? Walk the walk. Take your leave, pick your kids up from school, live your family values. You set the tone.
7. Establish programs to onboard moms returning to work after periods at home.
8. Encourage self-care by offering paid time off for "mental health" days.
9. Designate "moms only" spaces for moms who need to nurse or pump during the workday.
10. Offer empathy and compassion to working moms.

CHAPTER TEN

CARRY THAT WEIGHT

> Sometimes mom guilt is there for a good reason. Sometimes I really do need to intentionally shut everything out and pay attention to my kids. Sometimes it's true that I've been neglecting their emotional needs. Most times, though, mom guilt arises because we have false narratives about what it means to be a good mother.
>
> —Whitney Casares, @modernmommydoc

Ninety percent of working moms feel burned out, and I'm one of them.

I had a really healing and honest conversation with Jo Saxton on my podcast about burnout, and she gave a great summary of how this sometimes feels: "You are waking up more tired than you were when you went to bed. When you find that you are really short with people, where you'll become really exacting and you just gotta get things done. And your mind has no head space and your emotion has no heart space to feel except beyond the extremes… It's like chronic survival mode where you're not actually surviving."

A spa day won't fix this, mamas.

So why do we burn out?

Sometimes we're burned out on our own expectations.

Sometimes we're burned out on what's happening in the lives of people we love.

Sometimes we're burned out on motherhood.

Sometimes we're burned out on a job.

Sometimes we're burned out because we haven't said no to anything in months.

As I admitted earlier in the book, I've been burned out on motherhood. And much of this comes from my own expectations.

"How many of have been burned out on our expectations, on the mismatch of our expectations in real life?" Jo Saxton told me, talking about expectations of the grades we hope our kids will have, the athletes we hope they will be, the friends we hope they will have. "This is actually about us. It's actually not about our kids. It's about how we want to be perceived. And we will burn out on our expectations."

Spa days are great, but they don't fix the fact that you'll eventually have to go back into the fire of your life. So it helps to have someone at your side giving you some perspective, as Jo told me.

"The first thing I would encourage us to do is to not make that step alone where possible, because when you're burned out, your perspective isn't always the strongest…The thing I find helpful is to step back with somebody—whether that's somebody's your therapist or whether that somebody's a good friend of yours or a loved one—who sees the life you have, because you need to be able to pull back to see what is going on. Because you can't fix what you don't know. You can't fix what you can't name."

I was able to do this recently when discussing burnout with a friend of mine. She gave me a new perspective on the idea of saying no to things in your life: "When you say no to things, extract things, take things out of your life, what you do is you also take the joy out of your life and that's part of burnout. When I feel myself creeping up to the high level of exhausting, I realize that I have to add things that bring me joy."

She's saying that when we say no to things, we often say no to the things that bring us joy. This fuels burnout. So I took her advice and decided to say yes to something that would light a spark inside of me.

I like to try new things. Not long ago I was shopping with my daughter in one of the small towns nearby called Walhalla. It's a very small town set in the foothills of the Blue Ridge Mountains. As we were walking past one of the buildings, I glanced inside and noticed these trapeze contraptions hanging from the ceiling. It turned out this was a brand-new yoga studio that had just opened. I looked at the schedule and took a picture of it, thinking it might be something fun to do.

I had heard of trapeze yoga but didn't really know anything about it. I convinced my brother's then-girlfriend, who was a Pilates instructor, and my friend Desiree to go. We all thought we had found something different, and we decided to be spontaneous and adventurous. To go out on a limb and try something new. So I did it, and I had the best time. It felt good to push myself, to do something I'd never done before, and to smile all the way through it.

Trapeze yoga is essentially if yoga, Pilates, barre, and TRX bands all got together and had a baby. Imagine hanging upside down and being in a state of tranquility. That's trapeze yoga. It was so much fun. And I will be back.

Moms, take a step back to admit you are burned out. Talk to your friends and loved ones about the reasons why. Maybe simply saying it out loud is a start. Maybe you need to say no to the voice in your head that brings you down and acknowledge those expectations that you're never going to meet.

And maybe you need to say yes to something that brings you joy. Allow yourself to add those things that can bring unexpected surprises—like trapeze yoga.

PASSION AND PAIN

When I suddenly lost my job at ABC after nine years, it felt like it came out of nowhere. I didn't see it coming, but it forced my family onto a path that we wouldn't have chosen at the time. I can thank God now that we got what we needed and not what we wanted, but at the time there was a lot of pain involved. Even now, it's hard for me to reconcile lots of things about how it ended and why it ended…and because there wasn't closure. We came down to South Carolina just for a couple of weeks right before the pandemic, and we never left. I never got to pack up my office. Never got a chance to say goodbye to my loved ones and friends there. Never really found out why I was let go. It's like I literally just disappeared into the night.

Ultimately, I came to the realization that it's okay. I don't have to fix every single thing. I can be expectant and joyful about this next season and still be where I am, processing the pain of sudden change.

There were times when I wondered if my girlfriend was right with her response when I told her our family was moving down South. "You can't disappear into the ether," she said. But I recently looked up the definition of *ether*, and it surprised me. Britannica .com states that ether is "a theoretical universal substance believed during the 19th century to act as the medium for transmission of electromagnetic waves (e.g., light and X-rays), much as sound waves are transmitted by elastic media such as air."[1] Since I'm not an expert in physics, I couldn't make any sense of this, but reading it made me curious, so I looked up a few more definitions and found a simplified definition: "the space through which radio waves or computer signals travel."[2]

Maybe my friend was right. Maybe that's exactly what I've done. I've disappeared into the ether, into this space—this medium—for telling stories of working moms so we can enact change. And those stories can be broadcast in so many ways now. Letting the world know that 80 to 90 percent of moms are struggling with burnout and mom guilt. The reality is that moms are underpaid and undervalued in the workforce, and one in three are considering leaving the workplace altogether because it just doesn't work for them.

LIFTED HIGHER

For me, this new season has been about passion and pain. I'm going after my passion, which is giving working moms a microphone and beating the drum for them. But within that came pain.

I've had the chance to pivot and try something different, but that's also scary as hell. Leaving New York behind and heading down South was nerve-racking and painful.

But we don't have to carry that pain alone.

Too often we think we have to be a mom martyr. And we think that we can't ask for help. We think it's a sign of failure and weakness when we do ask for help. But you don't have to carry it all. The thing that has given me so much freedom is surrounding myself with a great community. We have to do that, with women in our friendship circles, book clubs, at work, or in our apartment buildings or neighborhoods who do life and help us out. Ask for help.

Let me say it one more time: Ask for help.

If I could invite you into the fight for working moms, the first thing I'd ask you to do is simple:

Drop something that you're carrying.

First of all, drop the perfectionism. A friend said this to me, and it really resonated. She said, "Paula, you're going to drop balls every single day. Keep the glass ones in the air and let the plastic ones fall." That really put things in a proper perspective. It gave me permission to drop the perfectionism as well.

Then drop something else. Whether it's your constant mom guilt, your expectations, your embarrassment over your resume gap, or your dirty dishes in the sink—just drop it. (You should maybe consider *setting* down the dishes, but if dropping those feels right, I say go for it.)

I know those shoulders are heavy, Mama.

You may have takeout food containers stacked by your trash can, a Jenga tower of meals you wanted to cook but didn't have time.

You may have an email inbox so overwhelmingly full that your heart starts pounding when you go to open the account—so you don't, avoiding the cacophony of voices vying for your attention and exacerbating the count of unread messages.

You may worry about your kids when you're at work and worry about your work when you're with your kids, all of which serves to compound your guilt, because "shouldn't" you be fully engaged with your family every nanosecond you're not at work? That's Mom's role, isn't it?

The calling of a working mom is great. The load, heavy. The stakes, high. In fact, I am confident that working moms have the biggest, hardest job on the planet. We also have the most import- ant, most wonderful job on the planet. But it's not a job we should continue doing alone. It isn't right, it isn't healthy, and it isn't sus- tainable. Just because we can carry it all doesn't mean we should. And if you look at the growing rates of depression among working mothers, you'll see the physical and psychological effects of carry- ing it all. I'm sure it's no spoiler alert when I tell you they are grim.

And *why* should we feel this way? Why should we feel as if we don't measure up? It all comes back to the introduction of televi- sions into modern American society. Back to June Cleaver and her fussy aprons and perfectly coiffed hair. It all comes back to fiction. Our measuring stick of motherhood is a mirage. She was never real. But the shame we feel when we aren't like June Cleaver or perfect Pinterest moms is certainly real.

Which is a shame. Because we're pretty damn incredible.

Our bodies and brains evolve with each of our pregnancies. We become more emotionally intelligent, more empathetic, and more compassionate. Our leadership capacity grows as we expand our multitasking skills to include the livelihood of another human being. We have scientific superpowers that have made us people worth hiring and people worth following.

But we can't forget men in this fight—not the ones we're raising or the ones we're doing life with. We've got a responsibility as mothers to train our boys into men who carry their share of household and childcare duties. We've got to increase the statistics of fathers who contribute *equally* to their children. The 46 percent or so we're reporting now is shockingly low and demonstrates just how far we have to go.

We can also invite the men we work with and work for to be part of the conversation. If we make them the enemy, we're only working on half of the equation. We need men to help hold up our banner, to speak for us in rooms we're not in yet, to champion us, hire us, and promote us so that we can reach down and bring up more women with us. Keep in mind that men are dealing with their own impossible social constructs—though not to the degree of marginalization that women experience—and they are not impervious to the same type of absurd expectations.

There is hope. There is a better way.

Let's carry our country into a new era of respect and support for working moms.

Let's carry our families into a happier way of living by tearing down fictionalized narratives.

Let's carry each other to a better way forward by refusing to let mom guilt convince us that we aren't the superpower-wielding badasses we've been called to be.

And, ultimately, let's remember: *We don't have to carry it all.*

ACKNOWLEDGMENTS

First of all—whether you're a mom, hopeful mom, brave male, grandmom, single mom, American mom, global mom—thank *you* for reading, believing, and supporting this message—our message!

To my husband and children: John, Caroline, JJ, and Landon—you are the lights and loves of my life.

John—you're my biggest fan. Thank you for believing in me, often more than I believed in myself. Never forget: you're my better whole. LOL

Caroline, JJ, and Landon—thank you for making me a mom. It's my greatest honor to love and be loved by you. Thank you for embracing and accepting this wholly flawed and imperfect mother who is just crazy wild about you and embarrasses you on the daily.

To my publishing team at Hachette/Worthy–you've believed in this message before it was even on paper. Daisy, Cat, Jenny, Kaitlyn, Stacey, Laini, Patsy, Kristen, and anyone I missed—you've worked so hard on *YDHTCIA*, and I couldn't be luckier than to be on the same team as you.

Daisy—you're one of the lone moms at the decision-making table in faith-based publishing. Let's change those stats! Thank you for your loyalty, persistence, and passion for this project and for wearing a thousand hats to make sure it was birthed.

Jenny, you stepped in at the last minute, essentially drinking from a fire hose—that wasn't easy. Thank you for your endless patience and for pushing us even more!

To single moms—you are *heroes*! And there are plenty of single mamas who poured themselves into this book. My writer and dear friend, Holly. I love you. This message is as much yours as it is mine. Daisy and Jenny—you're an inspiration.

I had the honor of interviewing some of the most renowned thought leaders on all things family and working motherhood—thank you for sharing your research and expertise!

To my small but mighty team at CARRY Media—Diana, Terri, and Jon. We are the #Dreamteam!

Terri—you're the one who HELPED ME THINK of the title for this book "YOU DON'T HAVE TO CARRY IT ALL!" Diana, you're the real MVP!

Tracy and the team at Rogers Cowan—thank you for getting this book into the right hands and hearts!

To my high school friends, college friends, the LVCOT, and Prayer Pads LLC groups (IYKYK) who push me to be better and encourage thought-provoking conversations around family and motherhood. You're the best cheering section a girl could ask for.

To my sisters and brother—Dianne, Mary, and Dan—I love you forever.

To my mom, sweet Carol Ann—your childhood stories for this book broke me! Don't ever stop singing to me or tucking me into bed when I come home.

To my daddy, Ed Faris, who is in Heaven but very much with me every day. Dad, #GoBlue!

Travis, your job wasn't easy—but it was essential! This book is so much better because of your hand.

If you read *Called Out*, my memoir—thank you. #YDHTCIA is my own called out story of founding CARRY and being called to something new and scary and exciting.

Releasing that book in April 2020, the beginning of the pandemic, was heartbreaking for a myriad of reasons. Esther, my literary agent, thank you for giving me the courage to dip my toes into the publishing world, again. Then again, this message had no choice but to come out, one way or another. I couldn't keep it inside!

And to Jesus for placing this calling on my heart, giving me the energy to pursue it, and consistently bringing the right people around me to both challenge me and cheer me on.

NOTES

INTRODUCTION

1. "The Motherhood Penalty," AAUW website, https://www.aauw.org
   /issues/equity/motherhood.

CHAPTER 1

1. Juliana Goldman, "It's Almost Impossible to Be a Mom in
   Television News," *The Atlantic*, December 4, 2018, https://www
   .theatlantic.com/family/archive/2018/12/motherhood-television
   -news-difficult/576913.
2. Jennifer Lewallen, "When Image Isn't Everything: The Effects of
   Instagram Frames on Social Comparison," *Journal of Social Media
   in Society* 5, no. 2 (2016): 108–133.
3. Brenda Marceline Yahraes, "Lived Experiences of Mothers
   Returning to Work after a Child-Rearing Hiatus," Walden
   Dissertations and Doctoral Studies 4116 (2017), https://
   scholarworks.waldenu.edu/dissertations/4116.
4. Ojus Patel, "Paying for Childcare Is Tough—Readers Reveal
   How They Make It Work," The Everymom, July 1, 2021, https://
   theeverymom.com/how-real-moms-pay-for-childcare.
5. Elizabeth Segran, "Why Work Has Failed Us: Because It's Making
   It Impossible to Start a Family," *Fast Company*, September 4, 2018,
   https://www.fastcompany.com/90223475/american-childcare-is
   -an-expensive-nightmare-is-it-fixable.

6. Segran, "Why Work Has Failed Us."

7. Drew DeSilver, "Rising Cost of Child Care May Help Explain Recent Increase in Stay-at-Home Moms," Pew Resarch Center, April 8, 2014, https://www.pewresearch.org/fact-tank/2014/04/08 /rising-cost-of-child-care-may-help-explain-increase-in-stay-at -home-moms.

8. "COVID-19 Jobs Day Reports," National Women's Law Center, September 4, 2020, https://nwlc.org/resource/2020-jobs-day -reports.

9. "Women Gain 63% of the Jobs Added to the Economy in March," National Women's Law Center, April 1, 2022, https://nwlc.org /resource/women-gain-63-of-the-jobs-added-to-the-economy-in -march.

10. Tom Spiggle, "The Gender Pay Gap: Why It's Still Here," *Forbes*, May 25, 2021, https://www.forbes.com/sites/tomspiggle/2021 /05/25/the-gender-pay-gap-why-its-still-here/?sh=2c5086b87baf.

11. Mellisa Holtzman and Jennifer Glass, "Explaining Changes in Mothers' Job Satisfaction following Childbirth," *Work and Occupations* 26, no. 3 (1999): 365–403, https://journals.sagepub .com/doi/10.1177/0730888499026003005.

12. Council on Contemporary Families, "CCF ADVISORY: Parents' Happiness Deficit: Must Parents Sacrifice Happiness for Meaning?" June 16, 2016, https://sites.utexas.edu /contemporaryfamilies/2016/06/15/advisory-parents-happiness -deficit/.

13. Amy Henderson, *Tending: Parenthood and the Future of Work* (Los Angeles: NationBuilder Books, 2021), 90–91.

14. Sundiatu Dixon-Fyle, Kevin Dolan, Vivian Hunt, and Sara Prince, "Diversity Wins: How Inclusion Matters," McKinsey.com, May 19, 2020, https://www.mckinsey.com/featured-insights/diversity-and -inclusion/diversity-wins-how-inclusion-matters.

15. Henderson, *Tending*, 6.

CHAPTER 2

1. Tom Lamont, "Dolly Parton: 'There's More to Me Than the Big Hair and the Phoney Stuff,'" *The Guardian*, December 6, 2014, https://www.theguardian.com/music/2014/dec/06/dolly-parton -more-to-me-than-big-hair-phoney-stuff.

2. Elisa Osegueda, "Dolly Parton and Carl Dean Renew Wedding Vows for 50th Wedding Anniversary," *Entertainment Tonight*, June 8, 2016, https://www.etonline.com/news/190615_dolly _parton_and_carl_dean_renew_wedding_vows_for_50th _wedding_anniversary.

3. Robin J. Ely, Pamela Stone, and Colleen Ammerman, "Rethink What You 'Know' about High-Achieving Women," *Harvard Business Review*, December 2014, https://hbr.org/2014/12/rethink -what-you-know-about-high-achieving-women.

4. Karthik Kumar, "How Long Does It Take to Recover from Delivery? (Postpartum Recovery)," Medicine.net, June 10, 2021, https://www.medicinenet.com/how_long_does_it_take_to_recover _from_delivery/article.htm.

5. Jonathan Watts, "Anti–World Cup Protests in Brazilian Cities Mark Countdown to Kick-Off," *The Guardian*, June 12, 2014, https:// www.theguardian.com/football/2014/jun/12/anti-world-cup -protests-brazilian-cities-sao-paulo-rio-de-janeiro.

6. Michael Lallo, "Karl Stefanovic's Sexism Experiment: Today Presenter Wears Same Suit for a Year," *Sydney Morning Herald*, November 15, 2014, https://www.smh.com.au/entertainment /tv-and-radio/karl-stefanovics-sexism-experiment-today-presenter -wears-same-suit-for-a-year-20141115-11ncdz.html.

7. Colleen Ammerman and Boris Groysberg, "How to Close the Gender Gap," *Harvard Business Review*, May–June 2021, https:// hbr.org/2021/05/how-to-close-the-gender-gap.

8. Ely, Stone, and Ammerman, "Rethink What You 'Know' about High-Achieving Women."

9. This data is based on an analysis of median hourly earnings of both full-time and part-time workers. Amanda Barroso and Anna Brown,

"Gender Pay Gap in U.S. Held Steady in 2020," Pew Research, May 25, 2021, https://www.pewresearch.org/fact-tank/2021/05/25/gender-pay-gap-facts.

10. Barroso and Brown, "Gender Pay Gap in U.S. Held Steady in 2020."

11. "At Work, Dads Get a Bonus, but Moms Get a Penalty. What Gives?" AAUW.org, May 6, 2016, https://ww3.aauw.org/2016/05/06/dads-get-a-bonus-but-moms-get-a-penalty.

12. Andy Kiersz, "This Chart Shows the Gender Pay Gap Extends All the Way to the Top of the Corporate Ladder," *Business Insider*, April 4, 2019, https://www.businessinsider.com/gender-pay-gap-for-top-corporate-executives-2019-4.

13. Naomi Cahn, "Women's Status and Pay in the C-Suite: New Study," *Forbes*, February 19, 2021, https://www.forbes.com/sites/naomicahn/2021/02/19/womens-status-and-pay-in-the-c-suite—new-study/?sh=76d0bb063762.

14. Robin Bleiweis, Rose Khattar, and Jocelyn Frye, "Women of Color and the Wage Gap," Center for American Progress, November 17, 2021, https://www.americanprogress.org/article/women-of-color-and-the-wage-gap.

15. Women in the World, "Indra Nooyi: 'I Demanded That at 5 O'Clock My Kids Were Allowed to Come to Work and Play Around," YouTube, April 12, 2019, https://www.youtube.com/watch?v=ggOPxDBZa24.

16. Indra Nooyi, LinkedIn post, February 14, 2022, https://www.linkedin.com/posts/indranooyi_mylifeinsnippets-activity-6899012358652735489-3sAB.

17. Jeff Steen, "Pepsi's Former CEO Shared the 1-Sentence Secret to Her Success as a Leader. It's the Opposite of What We've Been Told," *Inc.*, October 6, 2021, https://www.inc.com/jeff-steen/pepsis-former-ceo-shared-1-sentence-secret-to-her-success-as-a-leader-its-opposite-of-what-weve-been-told.html.

18. Indra Nooyi, *My Life in Full: Work, Family, and Our Future* (New York: Portfolio, 2021), 260–263.

19. Padraig Moran, "Want More Women to Become CEOs? Give Them Tools to Juggle Work and Family, Says Former PepsiCo CEO Indra Nooyi," *The Current*, CBC Radio, October 27, 2021, https://www.cbc.ca/radio/thecurrent/the-current-for-oct-27-2021-1.6226745/want-more-women-to-become-ceos-give-them-tools-to-juggle-work-and-family-says-former-pepsico-ceo-indra-nooyi-1.6227250.

CHAPTER 3

1. "Betty, Girl Engineer." *Father Knows Best*. Directed by William D. Russell. Story by Roswell Rogers. Season 2, episode 30. Release date: April 11, 1956.

2. Jost Amman, *The Brewer*, ca. 1568, https://en.wikipedia.org/wiki/Brewing#/media/File:The_Brewer_designed_and_engraved_in_the_Sixteenth._Century_by_J_Amman.png.

3. https://www.istockphoto.com/vector/old-black-and-white-engraving-of-giant-pumpkin-with-farmer-and-family-gm1187878772-335747160?phrase=19th%20century%20family.

4. "The Life of a Colonial Wife," History of American Women website, May 2008, https://www.womenhistoryblog.com/2008/05/life-of-colonial-wife.html.

5. https://www.istockphoto.com/photo/family-portrait-gm157675111-14772504?phrase=19th%20century%20family.

6. Stephanie Coontz, *The Way We Never Were: American Families and the Nostalgia Trap* (New York: Basic Books, 1992), 4–5.

7. Coontz, *The Way We Never Were*, 8.

8. Ingrid Ranum, "An Adventure in Modern Marriage: Domestic Development in Tennyson's *Geraint and Enid* and *The Marriage of Geraint*," *Victorian Poetry* 47, no. 1 (2009): 241–257.

9. Coontz, *The Way We Never Were*, 8.

10. Coontz, *The Way We Never Were*, 9.

11. https://www.istockphoto.com/photo/family-dinner-mother-holding-platter-with-roast-on-it-gmYPE_038-10000000171?phrase=1950%27s%20family.

12. Coontz, *The Way We Never Were*, 23.

13. "Joan Crawford: Hollywood's Most Glamorous Star," *Screen Guide*, October 1950, https://www.joancrawfordbest.com /articlescreenguide50.htm.

14. Coontz, *The Way We Never Were*, 28.

15. Michael Grossberg, *Governing the Hearth: Law and Family in Nineteenth-Century America* (Chapel Hill: University of North Carolina Press, 1985), 136–146, 170–177.

16. Coontz, *The Way We Never Were*, 34.

17. Brentine Daggett, "I Kept Up with a 1950's Cleaning Schedule for a Week—and I'm Exhausted," Apartment Therapy, June 10, 2019, https://www.apartmenttherapy.com/1950s-housewife-schedule -31000739.

18. Lisa Sharp, "A Real 1950s Housewife Cleaning Schedule," Retro Housewife Goes Green, March 10, 2021, https:// retrohousewifegoesgreen.com/1950s-cleaning-schedule.

19. Coontz, *The Way We Never Were*, 31.

20. Coontz, *The Way We Never Were*, 32.

21. Coontz, *The Way We Never Were*, 32.

22. Coontz, *The Way We Never Were*, 32.

23. Heather D. Boonstra, "Teen Pregnancy: Trends and Lessons Learned," *Guttmacher Policy Review* 5, no. 1 (2001), https://www.guttmacher .org/gpr/2002/02/teen-pregnancy-trends-and-lessons-learned.

24. Coontz, *The Way We Never Were*, xxiii.

25. Coontz, *The Way We Never Were*, 35.

26. Coontz, *The Way We Never Were*, 35.

27. Kara L. Barrett, "Victorian Women and Their Working Roles," master's thesis, State University of New York, College at Buffalo, May 2013.

28. Vivian C. Fox, "Historical Perspectives on Violence against Women," *Journal of International Women's Studies* 4, no. 1 (2002).

29. Coontz, *The Way We Never Were*, xix.

30. A. W. Geiger, Gretchen Livingston, and Kristen Bialik, "6 Facts about

U.S. Moms," Pew Research Center, May 8, 2019, https://www
.pewresearch.org/fact-tank/2019/05/08/facts-about-u-s-mothers.

CHAPTER 4

1. Claire Cain Miller, "Young Men Embrace Gender Equality, but
   They Still Don't Vaccuum," *New York Times*, February 11, 2020,
   https://www.nytimes.com/2020/02/11/upshot/gender-roles
   -housework.html.
2. A. W. Geiger, Gretchen Livingston, and Kristen Bialik, "6 Facts
   about U.S. Moms," Pew Research Center, May 8, 2019, https://
   www.pewresearch.org/fact-tank/2019/05/08/facts-about-u-s
   -mothers.
3. Elizabeth Kolbert, "Spoiled Rotten," *New Yorker*, July 2012, https://
   www.newyorker.com/magazine/2012/07/02/spoiled-rotten.
4. As quoted in Kolbert, "Spoiled Rotten."
5. Kolbert, "Spoiled Rotten."
6. Olga Mecking, "American Parenting Styles Sweep Europe," BBC
   .com, February 26, 2020, https://www.bbc.com/worklife
   /article/20200225-the-parenting-style-sweeping-europe.
7. HeHe Stewart, "Helicopter Parenting May Lead to 'Hothouse
   Children,'" Family Education, February 12, 2020, https://www
   .familyeducation.com/helicopter-parenting-may-lead-to-hothouse
   -children.
8. Emily Lodish, "Global Parenting Habits That Haven't Caught On
   in the U.S.," NPR, https://www.npr.org/sections/parallels
   /2014/08/12/339825261/global-parenting-habits-that-havent
   -caught-on-in-the-u-s.
9. Kathryn M. Rizzo, Holly H. Schiffrin, and Miriam Liss, "Insight
   into the Parenthood Paradox: Mental Health Outcomes of
   Intensive Mothering," *Journal of Child and Family Studies* 22
   (2013): 614–620, https://link.springer.com/article/10.1007
   /s10826-012-9615-z.
10. Pamela Druckerman, *Bringing Up Bébé: One American Mother*

Discovers the Wisdom of French Parenting (New York: Penguin Press, 2012).

11. "Paula Faris Reveals Why She Brought 12-Year-Old Daughter into Bathroom during Third Miscarriage," *People* magazine Facebook post, January 23, 2020, https://www.facebook.com/peoplemag /posts/10158982402478132.

12. Jennee Rasavong, "Science Says Working Moms Have More Successful Daughters," Lifehack, undated post, https://www .lifehack.org/344245/science-says-working-moms-have-more -successful-daughters.

CHAPTER 5

1. Quoted in Elizabeth Cantarow, "No Kids," *Village Voice*, January 15, 1985.

2. Robert G. Boling, "Deborah (Person)," ed. David Noel Freedman, *The Anchor Yale Bible Dictionary* (New York: Doubleday, 1992), 113.

3. Lowell K. Handy, "Huldah the Prophetess," in *The Lexham Bible Dictionary*, ed. John D. Barry et al. (Bellingham, WA: Lexham Press, 2016).

4. Eliza Griswold, "The Unmaking of Biblical Womanhood," *New Yorker*, July 25, 2021, https://www.newyorker.com/news/on -religion/the-unmaking-of-biblical-womanhood.

CHAPTER 6

1. Caroline Castrillon, "Why Women-Led Companies Are Better for Employees," *Forbes*, March 24, 2019, https://www.forbes.com/sites /carolinecastrillon/2019/03/24/why-women-led-companies-are -better-for-employees.

2. Ali Montag, "'Shark Tank' Star Kevin O'Leary: Women-Run Businesses Make Me the Most Money—Here's Why," CNBC.com, March 22, 2018, https://www.cnbc.com/2018/03/22/shark-tanks -kevin-oleary-women-make-me-the-most-money.html.

3. "Hickory Farms Acquires Wicked Good Cupcakes," Perishable

News, June 29, 2021, https://www.perishablenews.com/bakery/hickory-farms-acquires-wicked-good-cupcakes.

4. Castrillon, "Why Women-Led Companies Are Better for Employees."

5. "Research Reveals Half of Americans Want to Work for a Female Leader," Globe Newswire, January 25, 2018, https://www.globenewswire.com/news-release/2018/01/25/1305181/0/en/Research-Reveals-Half-of-Americans-Want-to-Work-for-a-Female-Leader.html.

6. Matthias Krapf, Heinrich W. Ursprung, and Christian Zimmermann, "Parenthood and Productivity of Highly Skilled Labor: Evidence from the Groves of Academe," Federal Reserve Bank of St. Louis Working Paper 2014-001, https://doi.org/10.20955/wp.2014.001.

7. Castrillon, "Why Women-Led Companies Are Better for Employees."

8. Stacey Delo and Jennifer Gefsky, "We Need a New Phrase for Stay-at-Home Mom," She Knows, October 14, 2019, https://www.sheknows.com/living/articles/2114919/new-phrase-stay-at-home-mom.

9. McKinney, "Strengthen the Momforce: Survey Results," April 2022, https://www.instagram.com/p/CdWrtTLODF_/.

10. Megan Gambino, "How Motherhood Makes You Smarter," *Smithsonian*, May 8, 2013, https://www.smithsonianmag.com/innovation/how-motherhood-makes-you-smarter-55995649.

11. Quoted in Gambino, "How Motherhood Makes You Smarter."

12. Craig H. Kinsley and R. Adam Franssen, "The Pregnant Brain as a Revving Race Car," *Scientific American*, January 19, 2010, https://www.scientificamerican.com/article/pregnant-brain-as-racecar.

13. R. M. Pearson, S. L. Lightman, and J. Evans, "Emotional Sensitivity for Motherhood: Late Pregnancy Is Associated with Enhanced Accuracy to Encode Emotional Faces," *Hormones and Behavior* 56, no. 5 (2009): 557–563, https://www.sciencedirect.com/science/article/abs/pii/S0018506X0900213X?via%3Dihub.

14. Quoted in Gambino, "How Motherhood Makes You Smarter."
15. "Emotional Intelligence," *Psychology Today*, undated post, https://www.psychologytoday.com/us/basics/emotional-intelligence.
16. Castrillon, "Why Women-Led Companies Are Better for Employees."
17. "Depression in the Workplace," Mental Health America, undated post, https://www.mhanational.org/depression-workplace.
18. Josie Green, "Who Invented the Dishwasher, Windshield Wiper, Caller ID? Women Created These 50 Inventions," *USA Today*, March 16, 2019, https://amp.usatoday.com/amp/39158677.
19. Jennifer L. Glass, Kelly R. Raley, and Joanna R. Pepin, "Children's Financial Dependence on Mothers: Propensity and Duration," *Socius* 7 (January 2021), https://journals.sagepub.com/doi/10.1177/23780231211055246.
20. Henrik Kleven, Camille Landais, and Jakob Eghold Søgaard, "Children and Gender Inequality: Evidence from Denmark," National Bureau of Economic Research Working Paper 24219, January 2018, https://www.nber.org/papers/w24219.
21. Quoted in Amy Henderson, *Tending: Parenthood and the Future of Work* (Los Angeles: NationBuilder Books, 2021), 91.
22. Bolanle Williams-Olley, "Raising the Bar," 2021, CARRY Media.

CHAPTER 7

1. Amy Henderson, *Tending: Parenthood and the Future of Work* (Los Angeles: NationBuilder Books, 2021).
2. Leslie Morgan Steiner, ed., *Mommy Wars* (New York: Random House, 2007).
3. Steiner, *Mommy Wars*, ix–x.
4. Steiner, *Mommy Wars*, x.
5. Quoted in Sylvia Obell, "Serena's Next Serve," *Insider*, April 13, 2022, https://www.insider.com/serena-williams-interview-cover-story-2022-4.
6. Linked at "Candace Cameron Bure Says Stay-at-Home Mothers Are 'Not Valued by Society,'" *Motherly*, November 5, 2020, https://

www.mother.ly/life/candace-cameron-bure-stay-at-home-mothers
-are-not-valued-by-society.

7. Katy Steinmetz, "'Stay-at-Home Mothers': Why We Still Use This
   Clunky, Outdated Term," *Time*, April 11, 2014, https://time.com
   /59807/stay-at-home-mothers.

8. Jessica Grose, "Why Do We Call Them 'Stay-at-Home Moms'?
   There Must Be a Better Term," *Slate*, March 26, 2013, https://slate
   .com/human-interest/2013/03/housewife-homemaker-or-stay-at
   -home-mom-what-should-we-call-women-who-don-t-do-paid
   -work.html.

9. Steinmetz, "'Stay-at-Home Mothers.'"

10. Grose, "Why Do We Call Them 'Stay-at-Home Moms'?"

11. Stacey Delo and Jennifer Gefsky, "We Need a New Phrase for Stay
    -at-Home Mom," She Knows, October 14, 2019, https://www
    .sheknows.com/living/articles/2114919/new-phrase-stay-at-home
    -mom.

12. Rosemary Counter, "Mom Shaming Is Running Rampant during
    the Pandemic," *New York Times*, September 10, 2020, https://www
    .nytimes.com/2020/09/10/parenting/mom-shame-coronavirus.html.

13. Henderson, *Tending*, 45.

14. Henderson, *Tending*, 24–25.

CHAPTER 8

1. Caroline Crosson Gilpin and Natalie Proulx, "Boys to Men:
   Teaching and Learning about Masculinity in an Age of Change,"
   New York Times, April 12, 2018, https://www.nytimes.com
   /2018/04/12/learning/lesson-plans/boys-to-men-teaching-and
   -learning-about-masculinity-in-an-age-of-change.html.

2. Jessica Bennett, "A Master's Degree in…Masculinity?" *New York
   Times*, August 8, 2015, https://www.nytimes.com/2015/08/09
   /fashion/masculinities-studies-stonybrook-michael-kimmel.html.

3. Quoted in Bennett, "A Master's Degree in…Masculinity?"

4. *The Kelly Clarkson Show*, April 29, 2021, https://www.nbc.com

/the-kelly-clarkson-show/video/justin-baldoni-wants-to-change-the
-way-we-view-masculinity/4352975.

5. Joanne Lipman, *That's What She Said: What Men Need to Know (and What Women Need to Tell Them) about Working Together* (New York: William Morrow, 2018).

6. Richie Zweigenhaft, "Fortune 500 CEOs, 2000–2020: Still Male, Still White," Society Pages, October 28, 2020, https://thesocietypages.org/specials/fortune-500-ceos-2000-2020-still-male-still-white.

7. Nathaniel Popper, "Paternity Leave Has Long-Lasting Benefits. So Why Don't More American Men Take It?" *New York Times*, April 17, 2020, https://www.nytimes.com/2020/04/17/parenting/paternity-leave.html.

8. Richard J. Petts, Chris Knoester, and Jane Waldfogel, "Fathers' Paternity Leave-Taking and Children's Perceptions of Father-Child Relationships in the United States," *Sex Roles* 82 (2020): 173–188, https://link.springer.com/article/10.1007/s11199-019-01050-y.

9. Francesca Colantuoni et al., "A Fresh Look at Paternity Leave: Why the Benefits Extend beyond the Personal," March 5, 2021, https://www.mckinsey.com/business-functions/people-and-organizational-performance/our-insights/a-fresh-look-at-paternity-leave-why-the-benefits-extend-beyond-the-personal.

10. "Paternity Leave: Why Parental Leave for Fathers Is So Important for Working Families," Department of Labor Policy Brief, undated report, https://www.dol.gov/sites/dolgov/files/OASP/legacy/files/PaternityBrief.pdf.

11. Noam Scheiber, "Victory for Fathers in a Parental Leave Case That Could Be a Harbinger," *New York Times*, May 30, 2019, https://www.nytimes.com/2019/05/30/business/fathers-parental-leave-jpmorgan-chase.html.

12. Quoted in Rachael Okerlund, "Why Don't Men Take Paternity Leave? And What Can We Do to Change That?" Parent Map, December 16, 2021, https://www.parentmap.com/article/why-paid-paternity-leave-men-statistics.

13. Juliana Menasce Horowitz et al., "Americans Widely Support Paid Family and Medical Leave, but Differ over Specific Policies," Pew Research Center, March 23, 2017, https://www.pewresearch.org /social-trends/2017/03/23/americans-widely-support-paid-family -and-medical-leave-but-differ-over-specific-policies.

14. "World Social Protection Report, 2017–19: Universal Social Protection to Achieve the Sustainable Development Goals," International Labour Organization, 2017, https://www.ilo.org /wcmsp5/groups/public/-dgreports/-dcomm/-publ /documents/publication/wcms_604882.pdf.

15. Samantha Fields, "Twitter CEO Paternity Leave Draws Range of Reactions," Marketplace, February 18, 2022, https://www .marketplace.org/2022/02/18/twitter-ceo-paternity-leave-draws -range-of-reactions.

16. Anders Dons, LinkedIn post, 2022, https://www.linkedin.com /posts/andersdons_barsel-maternity-paternity-activity -6892921242664390656-KaIl.

17. Quoted in Miranda Bryant, "Reddit Cofounder on Paternity Leave and Male Success: 'These Things Are Not Mutually Exclusive,'" *The Guardian*, January 29, 2020, https://www.theguardian.com/us -news/2020/jan/29/alexis-ohanian-paternity-leave-male-success -these-things-are-not-mutually-exclusive.

18. Stephaie Kramer, "U.S. Has World's Highest Rate of Children Living in Single-Parent Households," Pew Research Center, December 12, 2019, https://www.pewresearch.org/fact-tank /2019/12/12/u-s-children-more-likely-than-children-in-other -countries-to-live-with-just-one-parent.

19. *Fair Play*, directed by Jennifer Siebel Newsom, written by Eve Rodsky and Jennifer Siebel Newsom, 2022, viewing links available at https://www.fairplaylife.com/documentary.

20. Allie Volpe, "Splitting Chores Can Be Unfair. Here's How to Do It Equitably," *Vox*, June 20, 2022, https://www.vox.com/even -better/23161444/splitting-home-chores-unfair-equitable.

CHAPTER 9

1. Sue Campbell, personal communication with author.
2. Jon Zacharias, 2022, LinkedIn post, https://www.linkedin.com /feed/update/urn:li:activity:6911711185851621377 ?updateEntityUrn=urn%3Ali%3Afs_feedUpdate%3A%28V2 %2Curn%3Ali%3Aactivity%3A6911711185851621377%29.
3. Carly Martinetti, LinkedIn post, 2022, https://www.linkedin.com /posts/carly-martinetti-5949ab22_i-built-my-career-remotely-one -of-the-activity-6912427763723366400-9RX4.
4. Mary Beth Ferrante, LinkedIn post, 2022, https://www.linkedin .com/feed/update/urn:li:activity:6884622417562611712.
5. Amy Schwabe, "Working Moms of Milwaukee Recognized These 4 Businesses for Their Pro-Mom Policies. Here's What That Means," *Milwaukee Journal Sentinel*, April 12, 2022, https://www.jsonline .com/story/life/wisconsin-family/2022/04/12/working-moms -milwaukee-honors-four-businesses-pro-mom-policies /7198375001.
6. Katherine Bindley and Chip Cutter, "Workers Care More about Flexible Hours Than Remote Work," *Wall Street Journal*, https:// www.wsj.com/articles/workers-care-more-about-flexible-hours -than-remote-work-11643112004.
7. Sue Campbell, 2022, personal communication.
8. Alexis Reale, "How Countries around the World Use Flexible Work," Flexjobs, undated post, https://www.flexjobs.com/blog /post/countries-around-world-use-flexible-work.
9. Kasey Edwards, "I've Worked in Childcare for 15 Years. Here's How to Solve the US Childcare Crisis Once and for All," *Business Insider*, November 1, 2020, https://www.businessinsider.com/economy -needs-childcare-solution-how-to-make-work-2020-10.
10. Kristin O'Connell, LinkedIn post, 2022, https://www.linkedin.com /posts/kristin-o-connell-7b1a4528_supportedmother- productivemother-activity-6927320990603513856-Ofug.
11. "Vision," CPA Moms, https://cpamoms.com/vision.

12. Edwards, "I've Worked in Childcare for 15 Years."

13. Claire Cain Miller, "How Other Nations Pay for Childcare. The U.S. Is an Outlier," *New York Times*, October 6, 2021, https://www.nytimes.com/2021/10/06/upshot/child-care-biden.html.

14. Quoted in Jonathan Bastian, "American Parents Report Being 12% Less Happy Than Non-Parents," *Life Examined* podcast, May 22, 2021, https://www.kcrw.com/culture/shows/life-examined/copy_of_should-i-have-kids-children/jennifer-glass-interview-kids-economics-happiness.

15. https://www.kcrw.com/culture/shows/life-examined/copy_of_should-i-have-kids-children/jennifer-glass-interview-kids-economics-happiness.

16. Nicole Dow, "These 17 Companies Help Employees with Childcare," *Penny Hoarder*, August 15, 2022, https://www.thepennyhoarder.com/make-money/career/companies-with-child-care.

17. Kaylee J. Hackney et al., "5 Ways Managers Can Support Pregnant Employees," *Harvard Business Review*, January 12, 2022, https://hbr.org/2022/01/5-ways-managers-can-support-pregnant-employees.

18. Erin Spencer Sairam, "#ShowUsYourLeave Is Taking Over LinkedIn Feeds," *Forbes*, February 3, 2022, https://www.forbes.com/sites/erinspencer1/2022/02/03/showusyourleave-is-taking-over-linkedin-feeds.

19. Anumita Steinberg, 2022, LinkedIn post, https://www.linkedin.com/in/anumita-steinberg/.

20. Rebecca Keczynski, "Should Mother's Day Be a Company Holiday? According to Kendra Scott, Absolutely," *Inc.*, April 18, 2022, https://www.inc.com/rebecca-deczynski/mothers-day-corporate-holiday-paid-time-off-kendra-scott.html.

21. Kendra Scott, *Born to Shine: Do Good, Find Your Joy, and Build a Life You Love* (New York: Hachette, 2022).

CHAPTER 10

1. "Ether," Britannica.com, https://www.britannica.com/science/ether
    -theoretical-substance.
2. "The Ether," Longman, https://www.ldoceonline.com/dictionary
    /the-ether.

ABOUT THE AUTHOR

Paula Faris is an Emmy Award–winning journalist, speaker, best-selling author of *Called Out: Why I Traded Two Dream Jobs for a Life of True Calling*, and host of *The Paula Faris "Faith & Calling" Podcast*, where she talks to inspirational people about what they're called to do and who they're called to be.

Paula Faris has spent well over two decades in broadcast television, beginning with TV affiliates in Chicago, Cincinnati, and Dayton, and cutting her teeth behind the scenes by shooting, editing, and producing. Most recently, Paula spent nine years at ABC News, where she co-anchored *Good Morning America Weekend*, co-hosted *The View*, and launched the *Journeys of Faith with Paula Faris* podcast. She's reported on everything from politics, news, and entertainment to sports and faith, interviewing the likes of Reese Witherspoon, Tiger Woods, Joe Biden, and Kellyanne Conway.

In 2022, Faris launched CARRY Media with the desire to champion, advocate for, and celebrate working mothers across America. As the founder of CARRY Media, Faris runs her company from South Carolina while enjoying a quiet life with her husband, John, and their three children.